Just Us Girls

PETER LANG
New York • Washington, D.C./Baltimore • Bern
Frankfurt am Main • Berlin • Brussels • Vienna • Oxford

Wendy Rountree

Just Us Girls

The Contemporary African American Young Adult Novel

PETER LANG
New York • Washington, D.C./Baltimore • Bern
Frankfurt am Main • Berlin • Brussels • Vienna • Oxford

Library of Congress Cataloging-in-Publication Data

Rountree, Wendy.
Just us girls: the contemporary African American
young adult novel / Wendy Rountree.
p. cm.
Includes bibliographical references (p.) and index.
1. American literature—African American authors—History and criticism.
2. Children's literature, American—History and criticism.
3. American literature—Women authors—History and criticism.
4. African Americans in literature. 5. African American children—Books and reading.
6. African Americans—Intellectual life. I. Title.
PS153.N5R68 813'.540928708996073—dc22 2008014548
ISBN 978-0-8204-8132-6

Bibliographic information published by **Die Deutsche Bibliothek**.
Die Deutsche Bibliothek lists this publication in the "Deutsche
Nationalbibliografie"; detailed bibliographic data is available
on the Internet at http://dnb.ddb.de/.

Cover design by Clear Point Designs

29 Broadway, 18th floor, New York, NY 10006
www.peterlang.com

Contents

Acknowledgments

There are several people I would like to acknowledge for their support throughout the years that have led up to the publication of *Just Us Girls* and during the process of writing this book. First, I would like to thank my parents the late Earl Rountree and Pauline B. Rountree for their financial and emotional support during my college years and for occasional text editing. I would like to thank my dissertation committee at the University of Cincinnati: Drs. Amy Elder, Stanley Corkin, and Lisa Hogeland for their intellectual guidance. I would also like to thank the late Dr. Gay Wilentz and Dr. Paulette Brown-Hinds for their mentorship during my masters' and doctoral studies. Additionally, I would like to thank Sherwood L. McLamb for his patience and support during the final stages of completing my work. I would like to thank North Carolina Central University for awarding me a Provost Scholarly/Creative Productivity Initiative Grant which enabled me to finish the book. And, finally, I would like to thank Bernadette Shade and Phyllis Korper for helping me through the publication process and editing.

Introduction

> Once upon a time, I was a girl who wanted to write. I wanted to tell stories. I wanted to watch letters shape themselves into words on the page. I wanted to understand words and how and why they have impact. I wanted to communicate, to not be silent. I wanted, when I was older and understood the world a little better, to write toward a greater good, to create change through fiction somehow. The world was too crazy, and I wanted to tame it. I wanted to re-create it, and I wanted the historically invisible, historically poor, historically other people to win this time.
>
> —*Jacqueline Woodson,* "How Do I Come Home Again?"

The epigraph representatively describes the creative desire and experience for many African American women writers. Whether they are writers for young adult or adult audiences, they often seek "to write toward a greater good, to create [social] change through fiction." As an academic and fiction writer myself, I can identify with the epigraph's sentiments and do indeed hope that this academic work brings about positive change.

Just Us Girls: The Contemporary African American Young Adult Novel is inspired by my interest in how African American women writers have transformed the *bildungsroman* paradigm (the coming-of-age novel or the initiation story), rooted in Western aesthetics and interests, into an effective literary form of discourse where African American girls' issues can be addressed.[1] Many African American girls cannot fully identify with the characters or their experiences in Euro-American bildungsroman, and, consequently, African American women writers have produced their own novels to depict these girls' unique experiences in the United States.

More specifically, these writers' novels challenge the content and form of the typical western prototype and mold it to fit their own cultural/historical experiences: "[African American women writers] seek to discover, direct, and re-create the self in the midst of hostile racial, sexual, and other forms of societal repression, producing a literature not confined to the 'usual' Bildung model" (LeSeur 101).[2] These writers create female protagonists who must struggle against a racist society to develop cultural, sexual, and individual identities during puberty. Therefore, while a white girl's maturation process may be complicated because of her gender, she could be less likely to have to contend with social alienation because of her ethnic membership in the dominant cultural group. Young African American girls, on the other hand, face many more obstacles to the proper development of their identities because of their ethnicity, gender, and, sometimes, sexuality.[3]

One of the reasons Dianne Johnson wrote her seminal book on African American young adult literature, *Telling Tales: The Pedagogy and Promise of African American Literature for Youth* (1990), was to inspire other scholars to study "the interrelationship between Black children's literature and adult literature" (12). *Just Us Girls* answers this academic call. As a scholar of African American adult literature, my interest in African American children's and young adult literature was initially sparked by building literary evidence that there are many commonalities between young adult and adult African American literature. I have noticed that many African American women writers, irrespective of their audiences (adult or young adult), depict similar problems, to varying degrees, such as acculturation, broken or dysfunctional families, child abuse, community, identity, racism, and sexual orientation. Additionally, I have found that I can and do apply many African American literary techniques such as signifyin' to frame my analysis of young adult literature.

Eventually, however, I soon found myself asking a troubling question: Why are writers of African American adult literature and young adult literature dealing with many of the same issues? Since children's and young adult literature is universally thought to be an instructional instrument that teaches and instills cultural values and self-esteem in young readers, it would seem that the issues that concern young people would have been addressed before the children reach adulthood. Perhaps, because the root causes of these primary issues such as racism and sexism are so deeply entrenched in social, political, and economic institutions and society in general, these issues are never "solved" in literature or real life but are psychologically "managed" by African Americans. This answers my initial question. The function of African American children's and young adult literature is to teach young African Americans how to deal with these issues, not necessarily solve them, so that racism and sexism do not hinder their lives irrevocably.[4]

Marta D. Collier, in "Through the Looking Glass: Harnessing the Power of African American Children's Literature," posits that "African American children's literature [additionally] provides one way to support children of African descent through the process of developing a sense of identity given its authentic perspectives, flavor and [sometimes] illustrations" (235–236).

Whereas *Just Us Girls* is not primarily concerned with directly comparing African American adult and young adult literature, it examines themes and motifs that are often depicted in both. However, my focus is on the young adult novel and the unique initiation story/journey of female protagonists. I also utilize several "adult" literary theories and concepts to assist my analysis of some young adult texts.

Other questions I have begun to ponder are: What is the purpose of African American children's and young adult literature, what is the responsibility of writers of African American children's and young adult literature, and are the purposes of the literature and responsibility of the writers still the same in the twenty-first century? Historically, literature written for African American children such as W.E.B. Du Bois' magazine, *The Brownies' Book* (1920–1921), was a tool to bolster self-esteem in and to teach cultural heritage and values to African American children who were growing up during segregation and who were thus relegated to the margins of society.[5] Ultimately, the role of African American children's and young adult literature and the responsibility of those who write it has *not* changed over the years. For, "an African-American child born today will greet a world where racism, sexism, classism, handicapism, and a variety of other '-isms' continue to be subtly and blatantly at work" (Henderson 16). Further, African American children's and young adult literature is important to read and to study because it can teach all children racial tolerance and cultural diversity.[6] Linda Zoppa, in "Color and Class: An Exploration of Responses in Four African-American Coming-of-Age Novels," argues that "[t]hrough the vehicle [children's and young adult literature] it is possible that both black and white young adults will be able to transcend prejudice and racism" (176). This is a noble yet immense socio-political function for children's and young adult literature.

Whereas, prejudice and racism may or may not be transcended through the reading of literature, including such texts in classrooms and homes can help young people understand and possibly appreciate ethnic differences. Consequently, "African American literature, then, along with literature that reflects the lives of all the diverse cultural groups that make up this nation, must be an important component of the literature and reading program of all American schools" (Bishop 561). In contemporary times, the role of African American writers of children's and young adult literature is just as, if not more important today, especially in a world that often still reinforces negative or derogatory images of African Americans on television and movie screens and on radio airwaves.[7] In this society, "African American children need words that entertain, educate, touch the heart, and, ultimately, leave them hopeful" (Harris 539), and African American children's and young adult literature can assist in this particularly social and educational need.

When I began my research, I was surprised that even at the end of the twentieth century so few works of literary criticism analyzed African American children's and young adult literature. A number of bibliographies listed works by and about African Americans, but few articles and even fewer book-length discussions of their works existed. "One of the exciting things for scholars of African American children's [and young adult] literature is that its history is still being uncovered and written" (Johnson and Lewis 6). Therefore, I believe that more African American scholars must begin the work of rediscovering and studying works written for our children. I am talking about increasing the production of serious criticism in the field—much like African American scholars did in the 1970s when Zora Neale Hurston and her influential work *Their Eyes Were Watching God* (1937) were rediscovered by scholars and soon revered in academic and popular literary circles alike. This began a new renaissance in the academic study of works by African American women writers; as a result, more black women writers were and are being published. And, ultimately, the African American community and the world at large have benefited from reading these creative cultural products, thereby sharing and learning about their unique world perspectives. African American children's and young adult literature and its corresponding literary criticism have had and can continue to have a similar effect.

This level of academic scholarship is important because these books reach our children before and during their formative years and can better prepare them for life and the world at large. Nothing can take the place of parental and community teaching, but a book can open a young person's mind to the possibilities of a life of hope and possibility that she does not see played out in her own home or community. She can acquire the guidance and expectations that are needed to emotionally and psychologically survive and thrive in a society that rarely sees, celebrates, or validates her uniqueness —or even her existence. Knowledge of and access to these books is essential for these often marginalized, sometimes maligned, girls.

When I was a kid during the late 1970s to the mid-1980s, I did not have access to children's books written specifically for a young adult African American audience. I loved reading works by Judy Blume and Beverly Cleary, but especially as I entered my preteen years, I looked for characters who I could identify with, who shared similar life experiences unique to African Americans. I did not find them. I was not taught them. I did not read them. When I discovered the works of writers like Rosa Guy and Mildred Pitts Walter during my research, noting that they had been published in the 1970s and 1980s, I was pleased yet disappointed. Disappointed that I had not been exposed/encouraged to read their works. I do not want following generations to look back on their childhoods and think about "what could have been"?

Why weren't there many African American children's and young adult novels in my town's public or school libraries? Why did my teachers not tell me about them? Did they not know about these writers? Possible, and probable, reasons are political, social, and economic. I grew up in eastern North Carolina in a small town that did not fully integrate all of its public schools until 1976; taking this fact into consideration (*Brown vs. Board of Education* was decided in 1954), it cannot be surprising that highlighting African American literature in the school curriculum would not be a primary concern of school officials. Karen Patricia Smith, editor of *African-American Voices in Young Adult Literature* (2001), states, "While young adult literature has had a difficult time finding its way into the curricula of elementary and secondary schools, *African-American* young adult literature has had an even more difficult time" (xiv). This was the case during my own school years, and I fear, to a certain extent, that it is still the case.

However, I have to mention that my mother, a reading teacher, tried to fill the void. During the summers, she encouraged me to read works like *Pilgrim's Progress* (1678) by John Bunyan, a seventeenth-century English literature classic—because of her Christian upbringing and her education, which stressed canonized works. She also encouraged me to read African American non-fiction like the biography of Mary McCloud Bethune, my mother's hero. This was good for me, and I enjoyed reading about an African American woman's life. Even so, I would have liked more fictional choices as well. Perhaps, my love of reading and these experiences prompted me to write my first young adult novel, *Lost Soul* (2003), because I continued to see a need for more diverse African American children's and young adult literature.

Just Us Girls is an attempt to add to the literary criticism in a field that deserves more critical study. This book is a close reading textual study of prominent, although not exhaustive, issues and themes in contemporary (i.e., post-Civil Rights era) young adult novels written by both well-known and lesser-known African American women writers, written primarily from an African American perspective and primarily for, but not exclusively, an African American female audience. Representative works by Candy Dawson Boyd, Rita Williams-Garcia, Deborah Gregory, Rosa Guy, Virginia Hamilton, Mildred Pitts Walter, and Jacqueline Woodson are analyzed.

Each chapter investigates cultural, social, and/or psychological issues examined by the writers that are prevalent in the actual lives of African American girls.

Chapter One analyzes how these writers depict cultural and familial ties, particularly ties to a mother or mother figure, as necessary for the development of strong ethnic identities in girls. I compare Mildred Pitts Walter's work, *Trouble's Child* (1985), with its rural setting to Rita Williams-Garcia's work, *Blue Tights* (1988), with its urban setting. Although the two writers' protagonists are growing up in dissimilar geographical locations and social circumstances, both writers clearly illustrate how each protagonist struggles with, yet, benefits from learning about her African/African American heritage.

Chapter Two examines how African Americans have codified certain modes of behavior, dress, speech, and awareness as "black" to construct an "authentic" social and political group identity. In my study of two Jacqueline Woodson novels, *The Dear One* (1991) and *Maizon at Blue Hill* (1992), I discuss how this "authentic" group identity produces emotional and psychological "safe spaces" that enable the young protagonists to develop into healthy young adults. However, I also explore how "authentic" group identity can hinder the development of their individuality.

Chapter Three is an exploration of how and why these writers continue to discuss the effects of Eurocentric standards of beauty on the self-images of young African American girls—even in the post-Civil Rights era. In my analysis of *The Music of Summer* (1992), I examine how Rosa Guy portrays Eurocentric standards of beauty as a destructive power that still influences the minds of African American girls and causes ethnic self-hatred and intra-racial discrimination. In Chapter Four, I investigate how the African American vernacular tradition displays and has displayed African American cleverness, emotional strength, individuality, and inventiveness. In Jacqueline Woodson's *The House You Pass on the Way* (1997), I argue that the protagonist chooses to name herself after a legendary "bad" man in the African American folk tradition, Staggerlee, because her burgeoning sexual preference makes her feel like an outsider, a rebel, much like the folk hero. By identifying with the figure of Staggerlee, the protagonist gains emotional and psychological validation from her cultural heritage. As a result, she is empowered and feels secure enough to embrace her own sexual orientation.

I discuss an issue that is not often explored in African American adult or young adult literature—inter-racial friendships and relationships—in Chapter Five. Due to the historical and current practice of "racial" discrimination in the United States, we are still a nation divided along racial and ethnic lines for the most part. As a result, many persons of differing ethnic persuasions have difficulty understanding and trusting each other on a deeply personal level. And, because understanding and trust are key elements in the development of social relationships, inter-racial friendships and romantic relationships can be difficult to forge. I look at Jacqueline Woodson's *I Hadn't Meant to Tell You This* (1994) and *Lena* (1999) and Virginia Hamilton's *A White Romance* (1987) to examine the difficulties (adult prejudice and peer pressure, for example) facing young adults who choose to cross designated ethnic boundaries.

Chapter Six studies how writers depict death in their novels and, subsequently, help their young readers understand and deal with this aspect of life. I focus on two interlinked works by Candy Dawson Boyd, *Circle of Gold* (1984) and *Breadsticks and Blessing Places* (1985). In these novels, Boyd depicts the unique pressures girls experience in their homes and at school when a parent or a close friend passes away and how communality, typically present in the African American community, is key to the well-being of the children during their time of bereavement. Boyd illustrates this by showing the girls' need for emotional support from the remaining parent and/or a substitute figure (typically a woman), their peers, and other members of the community to cope.

Finally, in Chapter Seven, I analyze the effect of hip-hop culture on the minds of young African American girls. I argue that Deborah Gregory's *Cheetah Girls* novels demonstrate positive and negative aspects of hip-hop culture. For instance, although rap music and hip-hop culture were initially derived from the creative minds of urban African Americans, the music and culture have now been embraced by many youth of various ethnicities and nationalities. Gregory's novels reflect this aspect of hip-hop culture by embracing a postmodern sense of ethnicity. Her novels are populated by bi-racial characters and characters of diverse ethnic backgrounds, thereby, advocating for the need for ethnic tolerance to her readers. However, Gregory's characters also adopt the "bling-bling" lifestyle based on materialism often displayed by rap and hip-hop music artists. In doing so, I explore how Gregory validates these values and the consequential implications for young, impressionable African American girls.

In the conclusion, I speculate on the future of African American young adult literature for girls. In this postmodern moment, women writers of young adult literature for girls are increasingly stressing the multiplicity of identities through the content of their novels. And, while their protagonists must also contend with the pressures of "race," gender, class, and individuality, they must also deal with the more universal experiences that take place during the maturation process. Ultimately, *Just Us Girls* illustrates how women writers of young adult literature for African American girls reveal and validate the difficulties of growing up young, black, and female in modern-day American society, while seeking to improve the lives of their readers through literature.

1

The Function of Cultural Spaces in the Development of Ethnic Identity: Mildred Pitts Walter's *Trouble's Child* and Rita Williams-Garcia's *Blue Tights*

Community is defined by most scholars as a group of people with a common background, history, or with shared interests within a society. For people from the four main minority ethnic groups in the United States: African Americans, Asian Americans, Latino Americans, and Native Americans, the concept of community is especially important because it is a location of cultural affiliation and kinship. "The ethnic community functions as a refuge against the alienation of a different society. Ethnic communities provide a safety net where one's own kind can experience a sense of belonging. Ethnic communities or areas, therefore, maintain physical and social boundaries" (Bruhn 57). Ethnic communities are sites where young people learn about the history of their ethnic heritage, learn to identify with that particular culture, learn how to participate in their ethnic culture, and build a strong sense of who they are in the world based on their cultural identity. This role the ethnic community plays in the lives of young people is important because young people of color are often not validated or acknowledged in the dominant culture of the United States. These aspects of ethnic communities are positive attributes that typically instill high self-esteem in individuals in these ethnic groups.[1]

Oftentimes, these cultural ties are passed down through mothers or mother figures who share cultural knowledge with their children and ensure that familial and cultural heritage will be available to the next generation. However, at times these ethnic communities can become stagnant and can limit the potential of younger community members by privileging the past and tradition over adaptation and growth because of the fear of change. "Ethnic [community] boundaries exert powerful pressures on people of a given ethnicity to conform. Fellow ethnics who do not fit the mold are quickly identified. In this way boundaries bind members of an ethnic group to their culture and to each other" (Bruhn 57). While this strategy is important for members of minority groups to establish their own sense of self-worth in a dominant culture, it also can limit individual personal growth since those who do not conform to community customs may be marginalized by other members within the ethnic community. In this chapter, I compare Mildred Pitts Walter's *Trouble's Child* (1985) and Rita Williams-Garcia's *Blue Tights* (1988), analyzing how these writers depict cultural and familial ties within a community and how mothers and/or mother figures factor into the transmission of those ties to the female protagonists. And, although each writer's protagonists, Martha and Joyce, respectively, are growing up in dissimilar geographical locations and social environments, both writers clearly illustrate to young readers how the protagonist matures when each learns the benefits and confines of her ethnic community.

Robert Stepto's concept of "ritual grounds" is useful in analyzing the positive and the negative aspects of ethnic communities and, ultimately, in analyzing the way African American girls struggle to embrace and simultaneously move beyond the limitations of their cultural heritage and identity in *Trouble's Child* and *Blue Tights*. In *From Beyond the Veil* (1979, 1991), Stepto defines "ritual grounds" as "those specifically Afro-American spatial configurations within the structural topography that are, in varying ways, elaborate responses to social structure *in this world* [...] [T]hey serve as a spatial expression of the tensions and contradictions besetting any reactionary social structure, aggressive or latent, subsumed by a dominant social structure" (69). In other words, spatial locations, "ritual grounds," can have unique symbolic meanings. For African Americans, their communities can be "ritual grounds," sites where they are generally separated from the surrounding dominant society. The borders of the "ritual ground" are seen as barriers between "black and white spaces," which suggest an illusion of protection from white oppression. For example, during slavery black slaves lived on plantations, unsafe "white spaces," where they were exposed to physical and sexual violence. When blacks were in their slave quarters, designated "black spaces," they could participate in cultural activities such as storytelling, which created a sense of community and affinity. Even so, the safety of these "black spaces" could be undermined because of their vulnerability to the actions of slave owners; slaves could be raped, killed, and beaten while in the slave quarters. Therefore, the "ritual ground" is a dual, sometimes conflicted, space.[2] While I will briefly discuss the effects of white racism on the ethnic communities in *Trouble's Child* and especially *Blue Tights*, I will concentrate on the dual nature of these ethnic communities/"ritual grounds" within the ethnic communities themselves and the effects on the young female protagonists.

In Walter's *Trouble's Child*, fourteen-year-old Martha lives on Blue Isle, an island community off the coast of Louisiana.[3] In an interview with Shirley M. Jordan, Walter says that "*Trouble's Child* is a book about black people" (277) and a subset of black culture. In this rural island community, African Americans live by old traditional customs. For instance, girls typically stop formal education during their mid-teens and marry. "Martha knew that now, because she was fourteen, the pressure on her to get married would increase. Every girl on the island was expected to announce her readiness for marriage by the age of fifteen. This announcement was made by showing a special quilt pattern. Once engaged, a round of quilting parties was given in the girl's honor" (16). While Martha's closest friend, Ocie, unquestionably accepts island tradition and looks forward to marrying Tee, a local boy, Martha wishes to leave the island and to continue her education on the mainland—something that has rarely taken place. "No one that she had ever heard of had gone away from Blue Isle to high school" (16). However, Martha is different, and to illustrate Martha's difference, Walter writes that she was born during a storm. "[T]he people on Blue Isle believed that a child born in a storm was born to trouble" (14). The connection to the novel's title is clear at this point since Martha *is* Trouble's Child; for Martha, her "trouble" is negotiating the positive and negative aspects of her ethnic community. She says, "She felt now more than ever that she should leave this place. Oh, why couldn't she be like the others around her—happy with what she already knew? Satisfied, finished with school. No, she always wanted to know more" (18). As part of her bildungsroman journey, she will have to decide for herself how many of the community's traditions she will accept as her own and how many she will leave behind in the past.

To complicate matters, Martha, has lost both parents, the people who should be guiding her into adulthood. Her father died when she was five and is now "only a faint memory" (88) in Martha's mind. She is being raised by her grandmother, Titay, who is the main mother figure in Martha's life as her mother died during childbirth. "Martha remembered the story she had been told of how her mother had died when she was born on that stormy night. Titay had been forced to make a terrible decision: would it be Martha or Martha's mother who lived?" (88). She seems to harbor guilt because her grandmother, who was the midwife, chose her life over her mother's. She feels somewhat indebted to her grandmother, which makes her feel guilty for wanting to leave the island and resisting tradition.

While Martha does not want to marry Beau, an island boy who is interested in her, or anyone else until she finishes her education, she also knows she eventually wants a family because of the loss of her parents. "Martha had never known her mother. Her father, Titay's youngest son, had drowned in the Gulf before she was five years old. [...] Then she thought, *There's Beau and gittin married.* But she quickly put that out of her mind" (29–30). This quote reveals Martha's desire and motivation to establish her own family, yet the desire is not strong enough to immediately replace her desire for a different lifestyle and higher education.

A secondary mother figure is the island teacher, Miss Boudreaux, who lives on the mainland and travels to the island during the academic year. She is a representation of mainstream society in the text and to Martha. Martha looks to Miss Boudreaux for inspiration, guidance, and assistance. In the beginning of the novel, Miss Boudreaux is leaving the island because the summer break is starting. When Martha shares her dreams of higher education with Miss Boudreaux, she "look[s] at Martha with a sad smile, as if to say, getting away won't be easy" (16). Martha eventually appeals to her former teacher to help her further her education. Her desperation is obvious as she writes to her: "*Miss Boudreaux, Dear teacher. Please help me go away from here. I will work hard for just room and board and time to go to school. For the sake of my life, I have to go. I thank you very much*" (130). At the end of the novel, Miss Boudreaux is the one who makes it possible for Martha to leave the island and continue her education on the mainland. It takes a while, but she responds, "*Dear Martha, I am sorry that it has taken me so long to answer your letter. But you are a special person and I wanted a special place for you. I have found that place in New Orleans*" (148). Another mainlander, Hal, a student who is shipwrecked on the island after a storm, befriends Martha. She questions him about his life on the mainland and his experiences in college. Hal can see that Martha has an inquisitive mind, and like Miss Boudreaux, he encourages her education goals.[4]

However, because Titay is the island's premier midwife and most revered elder on the island and Martha is Titay's granddaughter, the community expects her to follow in Titay's footsteps. For example, after watching Martha perform a ritual dance at an important pre-fishing season ceremony, Walter writes, "The celebration lasted far into the night with everyone dancing, including Titay. Martha, catching the rhythm of the drums, rocked the party with her movements. There were whispers: 'She will take Titay's place, sho, and lead the festival'" (32). Titay agrees with the community and is impressed by her granddaughter's skills; Titay begins planning Martha's future. "They liked yo dancing. They all say how good you look and what woman you is now. So I think this time fo you t' start thinking bout yo life work. I'm old, Mat. Done kept the way o' this island. I gather herbs, wait on the sick. Peoples look t' me fo midwifin. I hop yuh ready t' take m' place" (33).

Titay does not encourage Martha's desire to leave the island and continue formal education—at least not until the end of the novel. Instead, she teaches Martha her traditional remedies and midwife skills to ensure that the knowledge is passed on to the next generation and to ensure that the island traditions will be preserved for the community as a whole. "You done finish school. Now you learn from me. We gather herbs and seaweed. We make the rounds, visit the sick. I'll learn yuh all you need know" (34). While Martha mostly conceals her own dreams, fearing to share them with Titay, she hesitantly yields to Titay's tutelage. She feels uncertain about Titay's expectations and her future as she carries out a particular task, gathering herbs for Titay. "Martha had never gone this deep into the woods to gather herbs and roots. She felt that this day in this new place marked the beginning of a ritual—an offering of a gift of some knowledge. Martha felt uneasy about being the receiver" (76). Yet, after all the doubts, Martha is convinced of her talent when she performs a ritual the day her friend Ocie dies. "As Martha assigned duties it was as if she were now trapped in Titay's ways. Her voice and her body movements were alien to her" (138–139). As her grandmother leaves her to perform the tasks for Ocie, the community knows that Titay is making a statement that Martha is ready, skill-wise, to take her place.

> It had been easy to forget all the questions, all the doubts, and act like Titay—to do things the way the women wanted and expected them to be done. There was no uneasiness, no fear, no reminding her that she had been born to trouble. That day she had not been trouble's child. She had been one of them: one of their own. They had been joined in that ritual with one thing in mind: the passage of Ocie's soul on its journey. (142)

On this rare occasion, Martha feels like she belongs to her community; however, she also knows that it is because she is accepting and performing the role that community members expect her to assume.[5] "The women needed her for their midwife, but they wanted her only on their terms: just like them—happy keeping the customs of the island" (125). Martha feels "trapped" by both Titay's and her community's expectations.

Martha also realizes that because her grandmother now trusts her to perform the ritual alone that Titay believes Martha is destined to take over her role in the community. Titay says to her: "T' do this work, girl, take mo'n knowin. Take being gifted. Tis a way o' livin. Yuh can't do this work wid jus yo hands n mind. You mus have the spirit. If it's writ down then anybody that read could think they know it. This is meant only fuh a few and you one o' em. I'll teach yuh and yo good works'll tract the nex one fuh the mantle t' fall on. You special, Mat" (76).[6] Knowing that her grandmother has such faith and confidence in her increases the guilt that Martha feels for not wanting to become the island midwife. To take Titay's place, Martha will have to relinquish her own dreams—ultimately, something she will not be able to do. In order to actualize her own aspirations, she must boldly confront her grandmother, her best friend, Ocie, and members of her community who all seem to fear outsiders and influence from the mainland.

Titay fears that Martha will permanently leave her island community if she continues her education on the mainland and will no longer respect the people and culture of Blue Isle. Additionally, Titay's desire to keep Martha on the island is based on her own personal negative experiences on the mainland. "I learnt m' trade heah but I thought I need know mo. So I want out there. I learnt a lot. But I seen plenty meanness and sufferin in lean-tos fuh my people near them main hospitals. The peoples woulda been better off at home. That's when I cided t' come on back heah and take care folks in they own houses" (95). Titay is describing racial, social, and economic discrimination, and she wants to shield Martha from that emotional and psychological pain by keeping her away from the mainland.

Titay's trepidation about the mainland and mainlanders is prevalent throughout the island community. Islanders want to limit their children's access to mainland culture and influence. For example, Miss Boudreax is a "temporary" islander who teaches the youngest children. She does not stay on the island and her teachings can only influence her students so much or so it's thought. Plus, the children's schooling only lasts until the mid-teens. Her influence is seen as limited, and therefore, non-threatening.

Another example is Hal. When he is shipwrecked on the island after a storm, Titay and Martha care for him while he is incapacitated, but the islanders, led by Cora LaRue, a woman who gossips and tries to take Titay's place in the eyes of the community, come to see if he poses a threat to them and island culture. "[T]hey wanted proof that their lives were not endangered by the stranger" (69). Eventually, the islanders begin to marginally tolerate his presence on the island. "Even though the people did not visit Hal's boat, or invite him into their homes, the women greeted him warmly, and the men welcomed him into their circle of talk" (75). Islanders are wary of the influence of mainlanders on their children and on their culture, and they resist change.

Martha even loses her closest friend, Ocie, because of her reticence to completely embrace community tradition. Ocie is deeply invested in island culture and has no desire to change it. She simply does not question it; instead, she embraces and accepts it as is. She has married at fifteen as expected and is learning island skills and traditions from her mother-in-law, Gert. "Near the chinaberry tree Ocie was enjoying the sun on that cool day. She waited for the younger girls to come to her to take their lessons: to learn to plait hair, to make pillows from moss and to protect themselves and smaller ones from poisonous snakes and plants. Ocie would soon be ready to replace Gert, who had supervised Ocie's training" (77). Unlike Martha, Ocie is pleased with her station in life. Unlike, Martha, Ocie is willing to only learn the adult island skills from her mother figure, Gert, and begin sharing them with the next generation of young people. In fact, Ocie takes it personally when Martha expresses a longing to leave the island community. She says, "Our way ain't good nuff fuh yuh" (90). By using the possessive plural pronoun "our," Ocie highlights her beliefs—that Martha wants to separate herself from her (Ocie), their community, and all that they represent.

Ultimately, Ocie thinks that Martha is rejecting her friendship along with island culture. Because of this she tries to hurt Martha by employing Cora to be the midwife to deliver her and Tee's child. Cora is jealous of Titay's position in the community and seeks to replace her in the hearts and minds of the islanders. "Everyone knew that Cora wanted to take Titay's place as the island midwife and caretaker but the women were afraid of her. It was rumored that she practiced hoodoo" (26). Despite negative rumors about Cora and Titay's spotless reputation, Ocie chooses Cora, and her vengeful decision leads to her death. Ocie's rejection of Martha and Titay out of spite has consequences; she dies in childbirth. Her child is now motherless and fatherless (Tee died earlier in the novel). Ironically, certain aspects of Ocie's young life mirrors Martha's mother, who also lost her husband to the sea and lost her own life in childbirth. When Martha performs the death ritual for Ocie, she is making peace with her old friend but also coming to terms with the death of her parents. This chapter of her life as "trouble's child" begins to come to a close. Of course, it is only after she has Titay's approval to leave the island that the chapter is finally closed.

Ocie and Martha's rift also affects daily island life and causes discord among the islanders. "The island was divided. Each eye and each ear was an antenna that picked up every gesture, every word. Rumors raced back and forth between those who supported Cora and those who supported Titay. There was agreement on only one thing: Martha had denied their way" (116). The island community is being torn apart. Only after Ocie dies and Martha performs the death ritual for her is the rift truly ended and the community reunited.

One of the best examples of Martha's alienation from her community, particularly the community of women, is a confrontation over superstition. On a typical shopping day, Ovide, the general store owner, has a hand mirror for sale, but none of the women will buy it. Cora voices the island superstition. "Yuh better cover mirror when it storm, and when somebody die too. If yuh don't they soul'll be trapped in that mirror and the mirrors' sho turn dark" (82). Martha feels humiliated, then angered when she sees how the women's fear puts a "smirk on Ovide's face" (82). Martha believes that some of the island traditions and cultural beliefs such as this one hinder the growth of her people as her reaction to the mirror superstition illustrates. She says, "Tis stupid t' think that bout a lil old lookin glass" (83). Lead by Ocie, who calls Martha a know-it-all, and Cora, who reiterates that she is a "child of trouble," the women dismiss Martha's comment. "The other women said nothing, but the hostility on their faces was frightening. They turned, almost as one, and left the commissary" (83).[7] In this moment of isolation, Hal, who witnesses the incident, offers support and pushes Martha to continue to question tradition and overcome superstition. "He whispered. 'Don't fear the mirror, fear *fear* of the mirror'" (84). Hal knows that Martha wants "to give to the women here some other ways of looking at their lives" (144) besides living under the fear of superstition.

In time, Martha can no longer deny her own dreams. Titay begins planning Martha's quilting party, which forces Martha to voice her distress. She openly confronts her grandmother, and Titay finally understands that Martha does not want to abandon Titay, her community, or her culture; she values it. Nevertheless, Titay also realizes that Martha does not want to limit herself to it either. If fact, she wants to bring back knowledge from the mainland to benefit all islanders. In the future, she could possibly be an even more effective leader and midwife for the island—if she chooses. Still, "Martha knew she could never tell the people that she was leaving against her grandmother's will" (155). Walter writes this statement to show Martha's respect for her grandmother and, subsequently, her community.

At the end of the novel, however, Titay explains to the community that she has agreed to let Martha go to the mainland and that that it is not a bad decision. Titay says, "Yeah, we hate t' see er go. Tis as though she saying she can't be happy mongst us. [...] But I'm gon gi'e er m' blessin knowin she's a good smart woman. She'll go and she'll see out there what I always say, ain't nothing new under the sun. All that's new sprang from the old" (156–157). Titay is "letting Martha go" to learn about the world for herself, which is part of any young person's maturation process.

It must be stated that often in young adult novels the protagonists' growing awareness of their identity and place in society coincides with their development from children into young men and women. This is also the case for Martha in *Trouble's Child*. She finds the process of becoming attracted to the opposite sex just as complex as her quest to establish her individual identity. As mentioned earlier, Martha is now fifteen years old, considered a woman by island standards, and is expected to marry soon. Like Janie in Zora Neale Hurston's seminal novel, *Their Eyes Were Watching God* (1937), Martha is aware of becoming a woman. Walter writes about Martha's burgeoning sexuality this way: "She felt herself growing, changing: long lean body now rounding, softening, her breasts no longer buds but blossoms. She needed no reminding: she was a woman" (100). Walter's description of Martha's maturation is strikingly similar to Hurston's description of Janie's maturation: "Oh to be a pear tree—*any* tree in bloom! With kissing bees singing of the beginning of the world! She was sixteen. She had glossy leaves and bursting buds and she wanted to struggle with life but it seemed to elude her" (11). The similarities suggest: 1) the power of Hurston as a literary foremother who has influenced and continues to influence African American writers of adult and young adult literature and 2) how female sexuality has often been described in literature through natural terms or comparisons.

Additionally, Martha and Janie are similar in another way. Many scholars have argued that Janie finds herself through her relationships with the three men—Logan Killicks, Joe Starks, and Tea Cake; readers watch as Janie grows from a naïve girl who listens to her grandmother, Nanny, to a wise woman who listens to her own heart and follows her own intuition. As a young girl, Janie's awareness of her burgeoning sexuality does not automatically ready her for "real" love/romantic relationships; only after Janie goes through her life experiences with the three men is she able to establish her own identity as a woman and a human being. For example, Janie marries Logan Killicks because Nanny wants her to be protected from male predators by being sheltered within the institution of marriage. Janie agrees because she is underage and must comply with Nanny's wishes but also because she innocently believes that, although she does not love Killicks at first, love will come with marriage. She soon learns that this is not the case. Later when she runs off with Joe Starks, she knows that Joe is not the true love that she has been looking for since sitting under the pear tree; however, she does believe that he is close enough to the real thing. She soon learns, however, that he is not because he tries to control her movements and behaviors during their entire marriage. After Joe's death, Janie meets and falls in love with Tea Cake, the answer to her pear tree epiphany. Janie thinks, "he looked like the love thoughts of women.

He could be a bee to a blossom—a pear tree blossom in the spring. He seemed to be crushing scent out of the world with his footsteps. Crushing aromatic herbs with every step he took" (101–102). Hurston returns to the similar natural imagery, "[h]e could be a bee to a blossom—a pear tree blossom in spring," to connect with Janie's initiation into love and sexuality at age sixteen. Tea Cake is undoubtedly *the one* for Janie. And, in this relationship, she experiences many aspects of a real romantic relationship, including jealousy, compassion, passion, and a deep sense of loss when Tea Cake dies.

Just like Janie, Martha is not a mature adult just because her body begins developing. Martha's sexual awareness does not prepare her for the choices that becoming a young woman will bring. Also, like Janie, Martha's reactions to the young men in her life signify personal change/growth for Martha upon deciding whether or not to establish a romantic relationship with Beau or with Hal. Each possible decision would create an entirely different life path for Martha, so she must choose carefully.

Most of the people in the community expect Martha to marry Beau because "[e]veryone on the island expected Beau to ask for her hand" (15). Martha thinks that Beau is a good person, but she does not want to be tied down in marriage—at least not until she finishes her education. Additionally, for Martha, Beau represents the status quo and island tradition. He does not seem to understand how Martha feels, why she seems to be dissatisfied with island life. Unlike Ocie, however, Beau does not resent Martha for her wishes. Instead, he still wants to make her his wife—even after he hears islanders say that Hal wants to marry her and will be competition for him. He says, "Have yo quiltin and I'll take my chance" (126). Martha tells him that she does not plan to marry any time soon—if ever—but wants to let him know that she appreciates his love and friendship. "I knowed you liked me, Beau, and I'm glad I got the chance t' hear yuh say it. I hope we can talk sometimes and be friends" (127). Beau agrees; they will always be friends.

Ironically, the island boy Martha seems to be interested in, is Ocie's boyfriend and eventual husband, Tee. Martha is not interested in stepping on Ocie's toes and trying to steal Tee away from Ocie; however, she does appreciate how Tee seems to understand her. On an occasion after Tee and Ocie are married, Tee hears Ocie harshly teasing Martha about kissing up to Miss Boudreaux, thinking she is better than the rest of the islanders and wanting to leave the island. Tee offers to walk Martha home and tells her not to listen to island gossip. "Women talk. But pay no mind t' that. You mebbe too good fuh heah, no? I think, mebbe, yes. And if you git a chance, go. It make you no better, no worse'n us, no" (39). Tee's words soothe Martha. Walter writes, "Martha fought back the tears. She was grateful that someone understood, but she didn't know what to say, so she said nothing" (39). When Tee dies in a storm while on a fishing excursion, Martha feels the loss deeply: "He had understood her longings. He had dared to tell her to leave the island. He had not thought her strange. Martha felt the pain of having no one to talk to now—no one who understood" (54). If Tee had been the interested party and not Beau, Martha's decision may have been more difficult. She may have found it more difficult to leave the island, or she may have actually married and gained a life partner who would have moved with her to the mainland and supported her desire for more education.

After Tee dies, Hal enters Martha's life and eventually takes his place to a certain extent. Hal is a college student who was shipwrecked on the island and who Martha and Titay take in during his recovery. Martha soon realizes that she is attracted to Hal but also to what he represents—the mainland and higher education. As mentioned earlier, like Tee, Hal encourages Martha to continue her education and to challenge island traditions, especially when they are not in her best interest. One day when she is collecting herbs in the forest, Martha is drawn to Hal, so much so that she seeks out his boat, the *Marraine*, despite island rules. She asks herself, "*Whym I so took wid this boat?*" (102). She is attracted to the boat because it represents the mainland and is a vehicle that can transport her there. However, it also is where Hal resides throughout his stay on the island.

When a sudden storm approaches, Martha is forced to call out to Hal for help: "Hal! [...] Hep me!" (105). She is literally seeking shelter from the storm on his boat, but she is also symbolically calling out to Hal to befriend her and help her move beyond island custom. She thinks, "In an instant she knew she could take shelter on the boat [which is anchored a short distance off shore]" (104). However, women are not expected to be alone with men; she defies this custom, in this case, out of necessity. Once the storm calms, Martha and Hal remain on the boat, talking about the island—its pros and cons, and Martha's desire to leave it behind. Even in this moment, Hal is weaning Martha away from island superstition and antiquated tradition. Hal says, "Oh Martha, my serious Martha. I'll do all I can to help you go. ..." (109). This conversation is reminiscent of conversations Martha had or could have had with Tee. Martha and Hal also share an embrace and kisses: "Again he held her face in his hands and moved to kiss her lips. Quickly she turned her head and his lips brushed her cheek. There was an invasion of yearning that she had not known, ever. Martha, pulling away, ran across the deck, down the ladder and swam to shore" (109–110). She fears that some of the islanders will see her alone in the presence of a man and tries to leave undetected. Unfortunately, Cora does see her and takes the opportunity to cause another mini-scandal for Martha and Titay by announcing that once again Martha defies island customs. But, the more important point for my analysis here is that while Hal awakens Martha's sexual desire, he also offers her emotional and psychological support like Tee did.

When Martha tells him about being born to trouble, Hal verbally reassures her: "We're all born to some trouble, especially if we're different" (107). She has an epiphany after hearing Hal's words: "'*Mebbe I'm boned t' trouble, but I ain't evil.*' The world came closer and she felt at ease, at peace with herself" (108–109). Hal normalizes and validates Martha's unique perspective on the world, her desires for self-improvement. Eventually, Hal announces that he is leaving the island to finish his college education and to become a marine biologist; he wants to marry Martha and take her away from the island. "[C]ome to Florida for nurse midwifery. I'll help you all I can" (145). Martha is tempted, but she ultimately creates a way to further her education on her own terms. She makes the adult decision to not marry Hal just to escape island life. This life choice is another example of her growing development into the adult world which culminates with her leaving the island with Titay's blessing.

Throughout the novel, Martha struggles to embrace segments of her own culture and to challenge others. She wants "to be proud and happy in Titay's way. But there were other things that she must know, see and do. She wanted to know how Titay's herbs worked and why. Titay only knew they worked and that was enough for Titay" (94). Martha wants to learn Titay's knowledge but also gain mainland higher education. While her aspirations create conflicts within herself and, at times, alienate her from her community, she continues to believe that there are ideas from the mainland that could benefit her community. When the islanders see her ritual skills, Martha reassures them that she is not rejecting her community; instead, she has embraced it. And, when islanders see that she will go to the mainland with Titay's blessing, Martha becomes a role model. She is showing other young people that there is more to the world than their small island and that it is actually important to explore other cultures and to learn other traditions. In doing so, she reconciles those conflicts for herself and her community, and in the process, she is developing into a mature young adult, who can express her individuality.

In *Blue Tights*, Rita Williams-Garcia's protagonist, Joyce, is also contending with positive and negative aspects of her urban community. She overcomes the harsh realities of being the daughter of a teen mother and finds self-worth through participation in an African-inspired dance troupe. Joyce is a talented student who is in advanced placement classes although she is often the only black or one of a few blacks in those classes; as a result, she often feels isolated in the courses. She is also a gifted dancer and takes ballet courses at her school. Her "[m]ama had been a ballerina, Miss Ballet Perfect, touring around the world on a real stage with a real dance troupe and with white fluffy skirts" (11). She would like to follow in her mother's footsteps and takes her dancing seriously.

Dancing is significant to Joyce because, in her mind, it creates a connection between her and her mother. Joyce was often left behind with relatives while Minnie, her mother, toured. She would visit between gigs; however, she and her mother were not able to strongly bond during her early formative years. Once she retired from touring, Minnie takes Joyce from the relatives and begins to raise her. Needless to say, there is distance between the two, yet it is obvious throughout the novel that they are making progress in developing a stronger mother-daughter relationship.

For Joyce, becoming a ballerina will bond her to her mother because they would have that in common. However, Ms. Sobol, the school ballet teacher, does not see Joyce as the ballerina type, "[s]lender, devoid of hips and breasts" (4). At fifteen, Joyce was already "from the neck down … a woman" (4) and has the physique of a developing black girl. Ms. Sobol denies Joyce the opportunity to perform in the school's ballet showcase, *Sleeping Beauty*, because "[she] wouldn't look right on stage. […] Not with the other girls. […] Dancers should never have too much of anything. […] It's distracting. […] It's not aesthetically pleasing to the audience" (4). By prohibiting Joyce from performing with the other girls in her class, Ms. Sobol is demonstrating her own prejudice and is saying that only a specific body type is "aesthetically" proper for ballet dancing. She is also making Joyce feel ashamed of her ethnicity.

If she had said that Joyce could not perform in the showcase because she lacked skills, Ms. Sobol would have seemed more objective and less ethnically biased. However, Joyce believes that she is excluding her because of the way she looks. Joyce expresses her anger at Ms. Sobol's bias in an internal monologue.

> *Like my body's a freak machine. Never mind the fact that I have a six o'clock extension. No. Never mind the fact that I have an arch. Hmmp. And turnout? One-hundred-eighty-degree action. I can do anything a ballerina can do. So she cleans it up by saying my butt is too big for ballet. What does that dry old heifer know about dance anyway? She get me sick. If God gave her a tail it would be all right. We'd all have to have one.* (4)

Joyce's righteous indignation is justifiable. Yet, Joyce is powerless to change this situation; she is not going to participate in the showcase. While this situation is a huge blow to her self-esteem—not being white—she also learns that she may have been able to be in the performance if she were light enough.

Cindi and Jay-Jay, girls of color, are allowed to be in the ballet showcase along with Merryl, the white lead. Ms. Sobol more easily praises these two girls while she openly criticizes Joyce in front of her classmates. "No! No! Don't' let your pelvis fall! Lift up ! Watch your butt! Look at what you're doing" (29). Ms. Sobol's criticism corroborates the other girls', particularly Cindi and Jay-Jay's, feelings of superiority over Joyce. She never criticizes or discriminates against them for their physical attributes. They possess lighter skin than Joyce, are popular at school, have boyfriends, and are from higher socio-economic backgrounds—everything Joyce is not.

Indeed, Joyce considers herself a "misfit" (9) and knows "she wasn't the finest girl in the school. She knew that. [She] was one of those girls that you would have to stare at really hard and say, 'if she'd only do this or that she'd be a fine, fine babe'" (6). To counter this reputation, Joyce tries to raise her social standing at school by associating with Cindi and Jay-Jay. She wants to believe that they are her friends even though it is obvious they simply tolerate her presence for laughs or try to avoid her all together. In an interview, Williams-Garcia says, "Class has a tremendous effect on relationships. People of the same class tend to have similar backgrounds, experiences, priorities. I think women seek others with similar educational background[s], family structures, parenting styles, goals, and interests to form their social and friendship bonds" (304). This seems to be the case in her novel. Cindi and Jay-Jay only tolerate Joyce; they do not offer her true friendship because they believe they are socially and economically superior.[8] "Joyce … is … aware of class status, or the lack of it among her peers. Growing up in the poorer section of a large city, Joyce's mother and her abusive step-father, work long hours to earn what is needed to survive" (Zoppa 182–183). The girls' condescension is not lost on Joyce, but she is still impressed with their expensive clothes and love lives and wants to be a part of their social group. "Joyce is … a person with very low self-esteem, and her behavior is always consistent with her self-perception" (Williams-Garcia 304). She is willing to accept their "friendship," in any form, because she does not perceive her own self-worth.

Even Minnie, unconsciously reinforces Joyce's negative self-perceptions. She says, "You fifteen years old and always in them dern sneakers and that ragamuffin sweater. You's too womanly to be dressing like some wild high school ditty-bop. That was fine last year, but you're in high school. A middle-class high school. You should be more ladylike" (44). Minnie's well-intended words are meant to help Joyce better fit into the high school social world, to be "more ladylike" in order to gain social acceptance at school. She does not want her child to be a social misfit. Her emphasis, however, that Joyce is now attending a "middle class" high school seems to suggest to Joyce that she must act differently than she usually does because something is wrong with who she is. Minnie's words, for the most part, can be seen as motherly advice; however, because of Joyce's fragile self-esteem, having her own mother say these words only increases Joyce's internalization of her "inferiority" in comparison to her peers.

While Joyce tries to gain self-worth through her association with specific peers, she also tries to acquire love, acceptance, as well as money and social status through her relationship with Sam, a married, thirty-eight-year-old man. Williams-Garcia says, "From Sam, Joyce gets that father figure. She wants to be Daddy's girl. She wants the love of someone who can protect her from the men on the streets, someone who can make her feel like a little girl. This older male figure represents this to Joyce. He knows this and pushes all the right buttons" (315). The "right buttons" are the correct choice of words here. Yes, Joyce is seeking a father-figure, and Sam takes advantage. She knows if she calls him he will come pick her up and will spend time and money on her—just like a father taking his daughter out for a day of bonding. Joyce thinks while on their secret rendezvous that she "almost didn't want to confide in him, but her need for his understanding overshadowed her insecurities. After all, that was the reason she'd called him. For some understanding. Sam always listened to her problems" (10). Sam is filling a "parental" void for Joyce.

However, Sam definitely does not see Joyce as a daughter figure. His own daughter attends the same high school as Joyce, but he "refused to name his daughter [to Joyce], as though his regard for the two girls would never relate in any way" (10). And, in his mind, they do not. In order to gain money and attention from Sam, Joyce "might have to let him touch her" (5). The implication here is intimate touching. Sam sees Joyce as a sexual object not as a "little girl" like his own; he would not believe that his own daughter would behave like Joyce. He certainly would protect his own daughter from the advances of a thirty-eight-year-old man. Although Joyce never has sexual intercourse with Sam in exchange for his attention, she does allow him some access to her body. Her actions with Sam further reveal her low self-esteem.

It is clear that Joyce's "community" at school and in her urban neighborhood is populated with people who either demean and/or who try to take advantage of her. However, once she auditions and joins the Kuji Je Tea Ujana Dance Ensemble, an African-inspired dance troupe that is a part of a youth employment project, Joyce is able to create a new community for herself, finds a spatial and emotional location where she feels she belongs, and increases her self-esteem in the process. Dejected after auditioning for and failing to get accepted into a prestigious dance conservatory, Joyce is wandering through the neighborhood when she hears "Da dum dum dum/da dum dum dum/da da dum dum dum" (57), the beat of a drum. The beat draws her, making her put "her life into a young drummer's calling" (57). The drum has drawn her to the ensemble's early rehearsal for a Kwanzaa celebration and is symbolic of African cultural heritage that will eventually bolster her self-esteem.

There she sees other African American dancers, women dancers, whose body shapes are similar to hers. "Joyce made notes on every other female. She watched them dancing with vigor and grace, uninhibited breasts and buttocks jiggling to the demands of the movements. Their shapes and sizes had such variety that she lost her uniqueness in the studio. She was just another dancer" (60). Joyce is able to witness African American women who are not self-conscious about their bodies. Instead, they are comfortable with them and have embraced them. By observing, Joyce can see that the women are displaying their confidence as women and as dancers—without inhibitions, negative self-consciousness. These women become role models for Joyce; she is one of them. As a result, she is able to concentrate on improving her dancing skills instead of concentrating on her difference.

Earlier when Joyce had auditioned for the prestigious Dance Conservatory, she is told that she has talent but must work on her technical skills before she could be considered for conservatory study. It makes sense that her potential has been stunted in the school's dance class. Joyce is so negatively self-conscious that she either cannot concentrate on Ms. Sobol's lessons and/or she does not work as hard as she needs to on her technique because she does not have encouragement from her teacher. Either way, Joyce finds guidance, acceptance, and tutelage in the Kuji Je Tea Ujana Dance Ensemble. In fact, after the rehearsal, Joyce learns that everyone who auditioned would be in the Kwanzaa celebration program. A fellow dancer, Tamu, tells her, "Everybody's in it" (62). In a spirit of communality, this dance troupe accepts everyone who is willing to dance. This troupe is rooted in African and African American communities' notions of communality—a focus on the group and not the individual. Many non-Westernized cultures, such as Native American culture, exhibit this mentality. The Kuji Je Tea Ujana Dance Ensemble is working within a different social paradigm—one of inclusiveness, not exclusiveness—like Ms. Sobol's class and ballet showcase.

Hassan, the troupe leader and choreographer, notices Joyce's talent. After showing the dancers a set of choreographed steps and moves, Joyce is the only one who seems to perform them to his liking. He asks everyone to watch her as she demonstrates how the steps and moves should be preformed. "They were all looking at her. The entire class. [...] And for the first time it felt wonderful to have so many eyes upon her. Not because her tail was round or because they were waiting to laugh. But because she was the dancer to watch. She didn't want to shrink away from their waiting eyes: Joyce wanted to dance for them" (74). Joyce has never been given such an opportunity in her school's dance course. She is in a "safe, black space" where she is being praised for her talent, not ostracized because of her body shape. Young readers watch as this protagonist increases her confidence with each dance step.

After several rehearsals, Hassan selects her as the lead dancer, the African Queen in the *Kwanzaa Suite*. Williams-Garcia is making a clear opposition here. Whereas Joyce is rejected from participation in the Western ballet, *Sleeping Beauty*, she "fits" and is the lead in the *Kwanzaa Suite*, an African American dance. Initially, Joyce is shocked that she has auditioned and won the lead. During actual rehearsals, Joyce becomes self-conscious once again, but this time it is because she does not feel as skillful as the other dancers and believes they notice her inadequacies. She experiences self-doubt. "Joyce's self-esteem is so low that when she gets the part for the African dance queen, she thinks: 'Oh, they're not going to like me.' Joyce will take anything positive and turn it into a negative because she feels ugly about herself" (Williams-Garcia 304). However, her new friend Tamu bolsters her confidence and offers her advice in handling her new position as a lead dancer.

> Joyce. There are a lot of girls who have been coming here for years working their tails off hoping to be noticed. You come in off the street, out of the blue, and you're already Hassan's girl. Now, we're not particularly vicious, but break your leg and see how fast we jump for your part. Sure, there's some jealousy, but you have to deal with it. The minute you act like you can't handle it the attitudes will fly up. Don't be scared no one won't like you. Not when you can dance like that. (76)

Joyce has admitted to Tamu that she has not actually performed "dancing like with technique" (76). Tamu encourages her to work on her technique because that will increase her confidence. She also persuades Joyce to take her school ballet class seriously because she "need[s] it" (77), and Joyce takes and applies the advice. At school rehearsals of *Sleeping Beauty*, Joyce watches Merryl, the lead, and how Ms. Sobol works with her. "No! No! This is supposed to be playful! You're making it look like something very hard to do. [...] Come now. Glissade, glissade, glissade, pique ..." (90). Joyce is surprised to hear Ms. Sobol criticize Merryl, whom she always thought of as Ms. Sobol's favorite student, the one who she always asked to demonstrate steps in front of the class. Through this observation, Joyce learns that every dancer must practice diligently to express the dance well.

Joyce also studies Merryl's technique. "Merryl, the dancer, not the show-off who was always twirling in front of the mirror. Joyce stood quietly, recording everything—the clean distinction of every step, the high feeling in the chest, the eyes that opened and focused" (90). Now, that Joyce is experiencing the pressures of being the lead in her own dance she can identify with Merryl. She no longer sees her as a "show-off" but a passionate, skillful *fellow* dancer who practices a great deal. In other's words, while Ms. Sobol's treatment of Joyce is in no way acceptable, Joyce now sees at least one reason why Merryl is often chosen to demonstrate dance moves for the class. Merryl is a *dedicated* dancer like the dancer Joyce is becoming in her own community, the ensemble. In this scene in the novel, Williams-Garcia states that she is "telling the reader not to trust Joyce; she can dance ballet, her teacher does not hate her, Merryl is not out to show her up. Joyce is just so good at jumping into her negative bag. It's comforting in there. Joyce doesn't realize the teacher is hard on her because she sees so much there" (320). I agree to a certain extent. Granted, Joyce has misconstrued some of Ms. Sobol's actions; however, Ms. Sobol's specific criticism of Joyce's body is an illustration that she is privileging Western body aesthetics. Nevertheless, Joyce begins to work more deliberately on her own technique. By doing so, she eliminates some of Ms. Sobol's criticisms and prepares for her own dance performance.

Joyce's performance is a success. As she dances, she connects to her African cultural heritage and to ancestral spirits through dance. Consequently, Joyce becomes more comfortable with her body and her existence.

> *And that's when they took her hands and said "come, daughter. Come child." The women in her back root, with warm and strong hands, broad hips, and loving bosoms. The Ibo and the Mali women, watching down at the Child dancing. Joyce heard the drum within her and stirred a mighty passion of feet and hips and head. And oh! the Child couldn't stop dancing, beyond music, beyond limit. "Leave her be! She touched by the dance!" they mused, spinning her, turning her, smiling down at the Child, who was touched by their spirit.* (121)

In these moments on stage, Joyce "hear[s] the drum within" and feels embraced by and a part of her cultural heritage. "[H]er level of black pride and her awareness of her African-American culture increases as a result of her experiences [with the ensemble]" (Zoppa 180). Interestingly, Martha in *Trouble's Child* also connects to her cultural heritage and the women in her community when she danced the pre-fishing season ceremony. The symbolic guidance and support of the ancestors bolster Joyce's dance movements, her cultural identity, and ultimately, her own self-esteem. Many people come to her Kwanzaa performance, including Cindi and Jay-Jay; they are all impressed by Joyce's dancing abilities. She has earned their respect, but she no longer needs or seeks it. She is now confident in herself and in her dancing ability and does not need their approval. She has found that support in her own community, the ensemble, and even gains open support from her mother. Minnie is proud of Joyce's performance and asks her where she has learned to dance so well. Joyce quickly responds, "From you, Mama" (122). Joyce has traveled full circle. She has sought connection with her mother through their shared love of dance and finally succeeds—not by sacrificing her own sense of self but by learning about herself and learning to love herself.

Additionally, Joyce experiences her first true love with J'had, the person playing the drum that initially draws her into the original audition. J'had works for the troupe in exchange for free karate lessons at the community center, but he does not really approve of the way the women dress or provocatively move. He has converted to Islam and tries to convert Joyce. She is tempted and attracted to J'had and wants to have a typical teenage relationship with him: "I just wanted to hold hands. That's all" (84). However, because of his strict Muslim beliefs, he believes that "a woman shouldn't just touch a man. It arouses his feelings" (84). He wants to treat Joyce with respect, even mentions marriage; she understands and tries to respect his beliefs to a certain extent. However, she would also like to participate in the same activities she has heard Cindi and Jay-Jay talk about.

For a while Joyce is willing to try to accommodate J'had's wishes so that she will feel and experience his love. She even begins to believe that she could adapt to Islamic ways and starts to believe in J'had's point of view. She tells Tamu, "once I start wearing the Muslim dress, people won't be staring at my behind or cussin' me out in the streets 'cause I don't tell them my name. They'll look at me differently" (101). Joyce thinks that she will increase her self-esteem and gain people's respect by taking on J'had's beliefs. Tamu must take on the mother-figure role again and "school" Joyce. "Joyce, people will see you as you want to be seen, when you start to look at yourself. You don't have to change your lifestyle to command respect. Just a few things" (101). Eventually, Joyce realizes this through her dancing, and she realizes that she cannot take on J'had's Muslim ways. (He, in fact, is no longer following the faith by the end of the novel, partly because Joyce kisses him and makes him think "impure" thoughts. Consequently, he believes he is not worthy of continuing in the faith.) More importantly, she realizes that she must raise her own self-esteem, find her own identity, and by her own method—dance.

The novel ends with Ms. Sobol asking Joyce to demonstrate some dance steps in front of class for the first time. She says, "'Yes! Yes! [...] This is what I've been trying to say—the line, the resistance, the natural pull and release of the contraction. This'—she beamed righteously—'is dance.' She smiled at Joyce. The one in the blue tights" (138). Joyce has now become the bench mark in the class, "a white space," by gaining confidence and a serious work ethic in her own community, "a black space." She has become empowered while in the "black space" because this is the location where she learns cultural heritage knowledge and can now remain confident even when she is in other spaces such as the school dance classroom. She does not "see Merryl on the side or Cindi and Jay-Jay to her back. Her focus remained in the mirror, at something wonderful opening up before her eyes" (138), herself. Joyce has completed an important part of her bildungsroman journey and learned many lessons along the way. And, so have Williams-Garcia's readers.

It also must be mentioned that when Ms. Sobol says, "the one in the blue tights," young readers can see the significance of this particular way to identify Joyce. The title of the novel is of course, *Blue Tights*, which refers to Joyce—her difference—in the eyes of her teacher, peers, and herself. Initially, the blue tights symbolically separate her from the others in the school dance class. "Joyce's uniform stood out among the whites, pinks, and baby blues, and blacks. She took class barefoot, wore navy blue stirrup tights and a mandarin orange leotard with an elastic belt around the waist that dramatized her proportions" (27). However, by the end of the novel, the blue tights signify Joyce's passion, talent, and uniqueness that separate her from the rest of the dancers, and Ms. Sobol can now see and acknowledge Joyce's technical improvement and dance ability.

Dianne Johnson calls Walter "a powerful griot," storyteller (129), and so is Williams-Garcia. They reinforce the value of young African American girls' cultural heritage and the special benefits of their ethnic community. However, they are not afraid to illustrate and question the limitations that ethnic communities can impose on young African American girls as well. Their bold literary choices empower their young readers to grow and challenge aspects of their own communities and encourage them to embrace the community aspects that fulfill their sense of cultural belonging and leave the ones that hinder their individual identity development.

2

Acculturation, Identity, and Ethnic Authenticity in Jacqueline Woodson's *The Dear One* and *Maizon at Blue Hill*

Children's and young adult literature often function either as a means to teach young people moral instruction or to entertain. When young adult literature is written for African American children, it often also assumes the responsibility of helping to shape a positive ethnic identity. "When a group [such as African Americans] has been marginalized and oppressed, the cultural functions of story can take on even greater significance because storytelling can be seen as a means to counter the effects of that marginalization and oppression on children" (Bishop 25). Many writers and scholars of African American children's and young adult literature believe that shaping ethnic identity is one of the main obligations of producers of this literature. Eloise Greenfield believes that producers of literature for Black children and adolescents should write books that "authentically depict and interpret their lives and their history; build self-respect and encourage the development of positive values; make children aware of their strength and leave them with a sense of hope and direction; teach them skills necessary for the maintenance of health and for economic survival; broaden their knowledge of the world, past and present, and offer some insight into the future" (21).

Jacqueline Woodson champions positive ethnic identity development for African American children while exploding the more traditional notions of ethnic authenticity.

While the majority of African American young adult novels depict protagonists who strive to develop authentic ethnic pride, Woodson's novels notably express a more postmodern philosophy. While her characters embrace a Black consciousness to develop strong cultural identities, Woodson sets herself apart from many African American children's and young adult literature writers by emphasizing the need for characters to develop strong individual identities. Woodson's characters complete their personal journeys only after they find a balance between their cultural and individual identities. This chapter examines two of Woodson's novels: *The Dear One* (1991) and *Maizon at Blue Hill* (1992) and argues that Woodson functions as a contemporary cultural and literary theorist as well as a novelist. By challenging notions of "authentic" black identity, Woodson creates a new perspective on ethnic identity in African American children's and young adult literature.

In a personal interview, Woodson talks about her reasons for writing for young adults and her role as an author:

> I want to open up a book and see myself in it and by extension, not feel isolated in the world. I believe it's important for young people to have this. [...] I don't exist as just a monolithic self and don't believe anyone does. There is a complexity to people and I want to get that on the page—the fact that there are ALL kinds of people in this world and they ALL matter. (Woodson)

Woodson's novels certainly address the issues that African American girls face in a postmodern context. The girls experience inter- and intra-racial discrimination and struggle with themselves, family, and peers to develop individual and sexual identities. Woodson's fictional worlds are complicated and sometimes unfair. One of the primary themes in the novels discussed here is acceptance of self and others. Woodson is mirroring the reality of many of the readers and possibly helping them identify with her characters' problems and solutions.

Robert Stepto's concept of "ritual grounds" is useful for my discussion of Woodson's novels and the ways her young female protagonists strive to balance individual identities with the perceived black collective identity, "a product of the group's history and experiences" that gives members of the ethnic group a sense of self-worth (Ogbu 173–174). In *From Behind the Veil,* Stepto defines "ritual grounds" as "those specifically Afro-American spatial configurations within the structural topography that are, in varying ways, elaborate responses to social structure *in this world* [...]. [T]hey serve as a spatial expression of the tensions and contradictions besetting any reactionary social structure, aggressive or latent, subsumed by a dominant social structure" (69). In other words, spatial locations, "ritual grounds," possess unique symbolic meanings. For African Americans, their communities are "ritual grounds," "black spaces" where they are generally separated from surrounding "white spaces." The borders of the "ritual ground" are seen as barriers between "black and white spaces," which suggest an illusion of protection from white oppression. During slavery, slaves lived on plantations, unsafe "white spaces," where they were exposed to physical and sexual violence. When blacks were in their slave quarters, designated "black spaces," they could participate in cultural activities such as storytelling, which created a sense of community and affinity. Even so, the safety of this "black space" could be undermined because of its vulnerability to the actions of white slave owners; slaves could be raped, killed, and beaten while in the slave quarters. Therefore, the "ritual ground" is a dual, sometimes conflicted, space. Stepto's concept of "ritual grounds" can also be applied to African American inner-city ghettoes as well as other ethnic groups such as Native Americans' reservations, Chinese Americans' Chinatowns, Chicanos' barrios, etc. Ethnic collective identity thrives in "ritual grounds" and is often derived from those who live in these spaces because "ritual grounds" are perceived spaces of cultural authenticity.

While "ritual grounds" are sites of community, Stepto argues that these psychologically safe spaces can also become areas of self-imposed exile, places where African Americans hide from the oppression they encounter in "white spaces." Stepto says: "[...] the grand tension [surrounding 'ritual grounds'] is that of self-initiated mobility versus self-imposed confinement: ritual grounds offer the exhilarating prospect of community, protections, progress, learning, and a religious life while often birthing and even nurturing (usually unintentionally) a sense of enclosure that may reach claustrophobic proportions" (68). The assertion that "ritual grounds," whether spatial or psychological, can hinder individual identity development is key to my discussion of Woodson's novels. For many African Americans, black collective identity, which is often based upon black working-class culture (the culture of those who typically perform manual and trade labor and are often less influenced by the dominant culture than the middle class), is a psychological version of Stepto's "ritual grounds," a safe "black space," where "blackness" is defined by specific "authenticating" characteristics such as speech, dress codes, ethnicity of friends, and culturally sanctioned extracurricular activities.

John Ogbu argues that ethnic collective identity is more or less an oppositional social construction because it has been forged under oppression (174). The black collective identity or psychological "ritual ground," therefore, possesses culturally "authentic" characteristics that enable African Americans to define themselves within and separately from the dominant culture. Spatial and psychological "ritual grounds" are present in Woodson's novels, yet Woodson highlights the dual, and at times, problematic nature of the concept by directly challenging "authenticating" characteristics of the black collective identity. She does this by depicting characters who do not possess these traits; consequently, young readers experience the characters' ethnic identity anxiety and eventually understand that prescriptive characteristics need not be sole guidelines for individual identity formation.

Black collective identity creates a safe space for young African Americans to develop strong cultural identities that foster positive self-images. But African Americans, particularly those in the middle class (generally salaried professionals who have appropriated values from the dominant culture), who are exposed to racially designated, culturally white experiences and surroundings, find themselves at odds with it. Woodson reveals this conflict between those who perform "authentic" ethnic identity and those who do not in several of her novels.

It must be noted that the culture of the working class is seen by many as the basis of an authentic black identity because of the belief that working-class individuals, and thus their culture, have been less influenced by the dominant culture than middle-class individuals. In *Authentic Blackness*, J. Martin Favor, argues that folk identity is the authentic black American group identity: "[I]f the uniqueness of African American culture lies in its folk forms, then the authenticity of the folk identity is privileged in the discourse of black identity" (4). During the Harlem Renaissance, many black scholars believed that: "[T]o know black culture, the artists or critic must know the folk; folk experience forms the core of the New Negro identity" (12). Literary works written during this time that explore this idea are Langston Hughes' *The Weary Blues* (1926), Jean Toomer's *Cane* (1923), W.E.B. Du Bois' *The Souls of Black Folk* (1903), and Zora Neal Hurston's *Their Eyes Were Watching God* (1937). Favor cites Houston Baker, Jr. and Henry Louis Gates, Jr., as contemporary proponents of folk identity because their work on blues theory and signification relies heavily on black working-class culture and the Black vernacular.

After the Great Migration, folk culture essentially became working-class culture because black farmers brought their culture with them when they moved into northern cities in search of work as factory, steel mill, and dock workers. With the rise of the black urban novel, ushered in with Richard Wright's *Native Son* (1940) and cemented with Ralph Ellison's *Invisible Man* (1952), black group identity becomes urban working-class identity. Blacks who for various reasons do not perform the authentic characteristics of the black collective identity are often seen as cultural traitors. In *The Dear One* and *Maizon at Blue Hill*, readers observe the difficulties that the young female protagonists, Afeni and Maizon, experience while learning how to develop cultural affinities and to negotiate between their perceived individual selves and their African American collective identities.

Although youth subcultures exist, Hans Sebald posits, "[T]here is no uniform subculture for all teenagers" (239). Sociologists contend that a single young adult subculture cannot exist because of the ethnic, geographical, and socio-economic differences among teens. Since identity is often related to ethnicity, kids from the main ethnic groups often struggle to establish individual identities separate from their ethnicity. What is interesting is that ethnic identity categories are often reinforced by both nonmembers and some peer members of the ethnic group, as is the case for, Charli in *Maizon at Blue Hill.*

Sebald states that each youth subculture has its own language or argot (270). As a result, for adolescents, the group's argot is important in distinguishing their group from others and in developing group and group-linked/dependent individual identities: "[A]cquisition of an argot means more than just learning a new vocabulary. It signifies membership in the subculture to which the lingo is indigenous. It promotes group cohesiveness and insures privacy" (Sebald 268). Because of a rich oral tradition in African American working-class culture, blacks have become masters of changing the dominant language to express themselves.

As a result of the popularity and mass marketing of hip-hop culture and rap music, contemporary urban black vernacular, argot, has become synonymous with African American youth. Urban youth have always had their own language, but with the mass exposure of hip-hop culture and rap music within and outside of the youth subculture, those black teens who use standard English are in danger of being identified as unauthentic. Middle-class youth and those youth who desire to achieve academically are often caught in the midst of this cultural identity conflict. Since the black collective identity is in opposition to the dominant culture, "in education, oppositional collective identity is associated with affected dissonance in the domains of curriculum (culture), language (standard English) and relationships with teachers and the school system" (Ogbu 174). Because many African American students perceive school as a "white space," activities and behaviors that are expected to be performed within the institution are considered to be opposed to the accepted behaviors of the black collective identity. Using Standard English is a major example. "[F]or some Blacks, [...] to accept the White definition of the right way to talk or behave is to accept White judgment that Black language and culture identity are bad and should be replaced by White language and cultural identity" (Ogbu 189).

In Pam Belluck's *New York Times* article, eighteen-year-old Fitzroy Dennison says, "[Y]ou learn to switch it off. When you're on the street, you speak Ebonics. [...]

When you're in school, you speak proper English. But when you talk too proper, your peers will call you white and say you're a 'cracker'" (15). Many academically successful Black youth have learned what their relatives have long known—it pays to be "bilingual." They use Standard English to succeed in "white spaces," such as at school and work, yet often use the black vernacular in "black spaces," such as at home or around other blacks to demonstrate their loyalty to the collective.

In *Social Cohesion and Alienation: Minorities in the United States and Japan*, George A. DeVos argues that African Americans are placed in a Catch-22 situation because of racism and the perceived collective identity. Ironically, in DeVos' terms, border shifts such as using the language of the dominant culture actually threaten the cohesion of the African American collective identity. When some members chastise others for not using the language of the collective, they are trying to protect the legitimacy and power of the group identity. In Woodson's *The Dear One*, Afeni Harris, comes literally face to face with this identity conflict when she meets Rebecca.

Afeni resides in Seton, an affluent African American suburb in Pennsylvania. She attends the private, predominately white Roper Academy and socializes at Jack and Jill, an upper-middle-class social club for young blacks, although she never feels completely comfortable in either the school or social club. She lives a somewhat sheltered existence shaped by socio-economic privilege. However, when Rebecca, the pregnant daughter of one of Afeni's mother's working-class friends, comes to live with them, Afeni learns about class status. Her displacement—whether physical or mental—from the working-class African American community hinders Afeni from learning and performing key codes of blackness, such as speech, which have been established by the African American collective identity system.

Afeni and Rebecca's first encounter displays the power of language in African American adolescent communication and how language indicates ethnic group affinity. When Rebecca enters the Harris' home, she is impressed by the material possessions. She says, "[Y]ou people are rich. I didn't know rich black people existed except on the Cosbys. But that's television" (Woodson *Dear* 45). Rebecca's comments reveal that she is unfamiliar with the lifestyle of the Harris home and does not associate African Americans with prosperity since she has not been exposed to middle-class blacks. The Harris' home and life, like the Huxtables', are not real to her; they appear to be television fantasy.

Therefore to Rebecca the people in the Harris home cannot be authentic, or real African Americans. In Woodson's *The House You Pass On the Way* (1997), Staggerlee loses her closest friend, Hazel, because of socio-economic jealousy.

After other African American girls tell Hazel that her family has money and that Staggerlee thinks she is "cute," Hazel tells Staggerlee that she had thought that she was "just regular, like all of us. But, you ain't" (Woodson *House* 24). Consequently, Hazel ends their friendship. In *The Dear One*, when Rebecca sees the Harris' fish tank and calls the fish "fishes," Afeni corrects her. Rebecca immediately becomes defensive because she feels Afeni is belittling her. Rebecca says, "Look! Just 'cause I'm in your ritzy little house [...] doesn't mean you gonna teach me how to talk and tell me what to do" (Woodson *Dear* 45). Rebecca's angry words reveal that she associates Standard English with the white and African American middle-class, not the African American collective identity. Rebecca also views the correction as a linguistic move by Afeni to show social and economic dominance over her.

When Afeni and Rebecca later argue, Rebecca exhibits the same defense mechanism but is more direct. During a discussion about money, Rebecca tells Afeni that she is not aware of the oppression of poorer African Americans in the inner cities. Their conversation reveals Afeni's misunderstanding of Rebecca's vernacular:

> Rebecca: Well, maybe not you, 'cause you the type people don't want to go near. My friend Cloe was like you. She didn't hardly talk to nobody. She kept all of this stuff inside her all the time.
> Afeni: What happened to her?
> Rebecca: She got stupid and cracked out.
> Afeni: She went crazy?
> Rebecca: Crack, Feni! C-r-a-c-k. Crack. It's little white rocks you buy in a vial and smoke. Hello?
> Afeni: I know what crack is. I just didn't know that's how you talked about somebody who was using it.
> Rebecca: Learn the language already. [...] God! You're black. Talk like it. (Woodson *Dear* 67–68)

Interestingly, "Rebecca [...] considers Afeni [...] to be a 'drop-out,' but a drop-out from the mainstream of black culture: an individual who chooses to identify with the white, dominant culture or pseudo-black culture reserved for the privileged population, and not with the black culture as currently perceived by American society" (Zoppa 185–186).[1]

Some of Rebecca's assertions are accurate. Because of Afeni's age (twelve) and because she has been sheltered by her social class from many hardships, she has difficulty understanding and acknowledging the social differences in the African American community. Afeni is vehemently against her mother allowing Rebecca into their house initially. She argues, "[O]ur house isn't some home for pregnant girls! This is my life, too, now and I'm going to decide who I do and don't want in it!" (Woodson *Dear* 14–15). Afeni's attitude reflects a certain selfishness and self-centeredness which is at conflict with the working-class African American community, which is usually communal. During this argument, Afeni's mother forces her to confront her selfishness: "[A]llowing Rebecca to come to live with us] is more than about what *you* want for once, Afeni! If you can't understand what being close to someone means and wanting to help them when they ask for help, then you have a lot of growing to do" (Woodson *Dear* 14). Afeni acquires empathy and a greater understanding of the complexity of black life through her interactions with Rebecca.

The working-class child forces the middle-class child to become more socially aware. Amanda E. Lewis suggests that individuals, including children, "most often [think] self-consciously about their identities in moments of confrontation with other individuals" (135). Rebecca teaches Afeni to empathize and to identify with working-class African Americans, enabling Afeni to begin the process of questioning black bourgeois values and her socio-economic status:

> Rebecca: You're just some rich kid way out here in the country. What do you know?
> Afeni: Seton isn't the country. It's the suburbs.
> Rebecca: Well, you don't learn nothing in the suburbs either. You stay stuck up in this mansion and don't talk to nobody. You just a little girl anyway. I don't care what you got say.
> Afeni: This isn't a mansion . It's just a house. And it's my house and you're in it. (Woodson *Dear* 64)

Rebecca continually mentions Afeni's isolation. This isolation has partly come about because Afeni's father has left the home and of the death of her grandmother. Afeni has also felt isolation at school; she describes student life at Roper Academy in this way:

> Roper Academy was founded by the Quakers and is private but not snobby private. We don't have to wear uniforms or remember the biography of some ancient-looking founder. And because it's in the middle of town, we aren't secluded from other kids who aren't students here. It starts at kindergarten and goes to twelfth grade, so we're supposed to be ace-boom buddies by the time we graduate. Caesar is my only buddy. (Woodson *Dear* 16).

Afeni's lack of friends indicates that she has had difficulties adapting to this predominately white environment. Ironically, "[W]hile Afeni never voices a desire to identify with characteristics of the white world for the purpose of gaining acceptance of her white peers, her attending the private school, [her use of Standard

English], and attaining superior grades are perceived by [Rebecca] as an attempt at white bonding" (Zoppa 179).

Woodson's *Maizon at Blue Hill,* the second novel in the trilogy *Last Summer with Maizon* (1990), *Maizon at Blue Hill,* and *Between Madison and Palmetto* (1993) further illustrates the effects of acculturation on young girls. Maizon, a young girl from a working-class African American neighborhood in Brooklyn, is reluctant to leave home and attend a boarding-school, the predominately white Blue Hill Academy. Her grandmother encourages her to leave the black "ritual ground" because she wants her to "experience difference" (Woodson *Maizon* 5). Her grandmother says, "[E]verybody wants a safe place. For me it was Colorado on the reservation. But I knew if I wanted to grow I had to leave. Madison Street is your safe place. But if you stay here too long, you'll begin to think that this is all there is to life" (*Maizon* 5). Here, her grandmother expresses the dangers of depending on the "ritual ground," hiding there for security, and not facing life in a more racially diverse society.

At Blue Hill Academy, most of the girls are from affluent families, including the four other black girls. Maizon excels academically but never feels as if she belongs. She "is unhappy in the cold and inhospitable environment of the private school and reluctant to let her loved ones know" (Bishop *Books* 617). Maizon experiences alienation at Blue Hill because of the fear bred by ignorance and racism in the white girls and because of the protective separatist actions of the African American girls. When Maizon decides to join the debate club, Sybil, a white girl who has invited her to come to the organizational meeting, asks her, in front of the all-white group, what it is like to be an African American at Blue Hill. Mazion says, "I stared hard into Sybil's eyes, all the while knowing that what I was doing was wrong for me. What I saw there was Sybil's own fear of me and this made me madder than I had ever been" (Woodson *Maizon* 90). Maizon resents being made to feel self-conscious and different; she leaves the school in search of a more familiar "black space," Madison Street.

Maizon directly confronts the girls and voices her concerns; black and white girls directly talk about how racism affects their relationships in many of Woodson's novels.[2] By having her characters confront this issue in their dialogue, Woodson stresses her belief that friendships are difficult and that societal ills influence them. In a personal interview, Woodson says, "[T]rue friendship is complex and rewarding and difficult. Everyone knows that. Young people truly know that. [...] The novels talk about friendship but they [are] talking about bigger themes in talking about friendship—race, class, sexuality, family, etc." Woodson has her characters actually discuss these issues since her readers are likely experiencing similar problems.

After this incident, Maizon is wary of friendships with white girls, including her roommate, Sandy. They eventually become friends but not close: "[T]here was still a cautious distance between us. Sandy was never sure when I'd get in one of my moods and not speak to her and I was always cautious that she'd get with her friends and pretend she didn't know me" (Woodson *Maizon* 118). There is an emotional boundary that is never crossed. Because of racism Maizon feels she cannot trust a white girl enough to consider her a close friend.[3]

When Maizon returns home in, *Between Madison and Palmetto*, she also has difficulty making friends with Caroline, a white girl, who has moved with her family into a condominium that has been built in the newly integrated neighborhood. Margaret, Maizon's friend from the old neighborhood, does not have as much difficulty making friends with Caroline because she has not experienced the negativity that Maizon has had at Blue Hill. Ironically, Margaret who remains on Madison Street, the "ritual ground," and does not have close contact with white girls is better suited to interact with Caroline than Maizon. Because Margaret has not been disconnected from Madison Street and her family, she maintains her sense of self and community. Margaret is able to interact with Caroline, in this case the "other," because she is psychologically situated in a place of love and support. Maizon, on the other hand, has been separated from Madison Street and the emotional support of her grandmother and community, thereby rendering the influence of "ritual ground" less effective.

In comparing her situation to Margaret's, Maizon even says, "Margaret had something I didn't have anymore. A belonging" (Woodson *Maizon* 99). When Maizon encounters the white girls at the boarding school, she is at a disadvantage because she is in their "white space," not her community's "black space." At Blue Hill, Maizon experiences "otherness," while Margaret remains protected on Madison Street, where Caroline is the perceived "other." Consequently, Maizon develops an aversion for white girls, and Margaret does not. However, after Maizon has been in her community for a while and gets to know Caroline, the two girls become good friends. By comparing Maizon and Margaret's reaction to Caroline, Woodson reveals the positive benefits of "ritual grounds."

In *Maizon at Blue Hill*, the other African American girls—Charli, Marie, and Sheila—who attend the boarding school have already learned difficult lessons about racism and friendship. Charli tells Maizon about how a white friend she thought was a close friend had not acknowledged her when she called her over vacation. Because of such negative experiences at school, the girls do not feel like a part of the school community. The girls say they attend Blue Hill just to receive an education and to get into Ivy League universities or top African American colleges like Spelman, but not to make friends. Since there are no all-black boarding schools,

Shelia says, "[W]e come here, find a few black people to hang with, and protect ourselves" (Woodson *Maizon* 94). They choose only to socialize with one another and join the same organizations. At school, a "white space," the girls create a "black space," their own circle of friends, to protect themselves. Using characteristics of the African American collective identity as a basis, they determine whom to allow into their circle and whom to exclude. According to Simpson, "[i]n majority-white environments, many black students are likely to embrace a black identity to protect themselves from feeling that they do not belong. Solidarity with other black students then becomes an essential survival tool" (148).

Charli, the most friendly of the three, invites Maizon to join them when she arrives at Blue Hill. Later in the semester when Maizon expresses a desire to belong to the school community by joining organizations and to socialize with girls of all ethnicities, including whites, these girls warn her that she will never belong at Blue Hill because it is a white institution. They stop speaking to her; their friendship ends, and she begins to feel completely isolated. Maizon does not violate codes of blackness such as speech or dress that are attributed to the African American collective identity. However, by wanting to associate with girls of all "races," she is perceived by the girls to be rejecting their separatist sensibility, which is present in the African American collective identity.

Pauli is a biracial girl who has also been ostracized by the three black girls because she has befriended whites. Earlier in the novel, when Maizon asks the girls about Pauli, Charli says, "'[I]t doesn't matter.' [...] 'Pauli doesn't hang with sisters'" (Woodson *Maizon* 56). Later, when Maizon wants to become involved with other girls, Charli even warns her, "[D]on't go turning a Pauli on us" (Woodson *Maizon* 83).

When Maizon approaches her, Pauli is suspicious. Maizon learns that, like herself, Pauli wants to belong to the entire school community, and her move toward individuality has cost her black friendships. She says, "[I] don't know what they told you about me being an 'oreo' or whatever they call me. But when I first came here, I wanted to be on the math team really bad, even if it meant that I'd be the only black girl on it. And they gave me ultimatums too. [...] But I had to find my own way here" (Woodson *Maizon* 113–114).

Pauli's situation is complicated by the fact that she has been living with her white father, who has not encouraged her to establish an African American identity. As Charli rightly notes, and Afeni soon realizes, Pauli lacks a black consciousness and chooses not to attend black cultural activities during Black History Month or to participate in Kwanzaa at school. Ultimately, she feels as if she is "stuck between two worlds" (Woodson *Maizon* 116), and she is not ready to confront her situation.[4] Pauli does not see herself as an authentic member of the black or white community: "[S]ometimes, neither world [ethnic community] is very inviting" (Woodson *Maizon* 116).

With the character of Pauli, Woodson ventures into new territory and complicates the issue of identity by including biracial girls. Pauli not only has to contend with her black and individual identities but also her white identity. She does not feel authentically white or black because of her mixed heritage and, therefore, does not feel fully culturally situated in either ethnic group.

Pauli says, "[F]irst I denied the black part of myself to try to fit, then the white part of me. Then I just accepted both. I mean, I *am* black and white [...]. I can't choose between the two" (Woodson *Maizon* 115). At the end of the novel, Maizon wonders "what would happen to Pauli [...] would [she] one day wake up and find herself lost" (Woodson *Maizon* 130). Maizon's thoughts reveal that, like Pauli, she believes that having a black consciousness should not limit her ability to be an individual, but she also believes that a black consciousness is important for establishing her cultural identity. Both girls, ultimately, reject the black community at school because of its restrictive nature. They want to be in the system yet also to be able to make social connections outside of the system.[5]

Maizon leaves Blue Hill after one semester and returns to her urban community, a "ritual ground," in search of a place where she can "fit in being both black and smart" (Woodon *Maizon* 126). Maizon does not feel as if she belongs at Blue Hill and seeks security in a more familiar environment. Maizon admits to herself that she returns home because "it was me who had isolated myself at Blue Hill, that it was me, closing myself off from everyone and everything because I didn't belong to any of it" (Woodson *Maizon* 128). Instead of choosing to become exclusively a part of the white group like Pauli or a part of the black group like Charli, Maizon chooses to be on her own because she does not believe she fits into just one of the groups. If the binary black/white groupings which white racism and the perceived African American collective identity create were not present, Maizon would feel more comfortable moving back and forth between the two.

Ironically, while Pauli is excluded from the black girls' group because she decides to also befriend white girls, she seems to be accepted by white girls: "Pauli [...] was laughing with the group of white girls sitting at her table. They stared at her adoringly" (Woodson *Maizon* 56). The first time Maizon sees Pauli she knows that she is black, so we can assume that she may have a fair complexion but possesses some obvious physical features that suggest her ethnicity. Therefore, it can be assumed that the white girls also view her as black but accept her. However, they may also know that she is biracial and that she has been raised by her white father; under these circumstances, the white girls may not perceive her as much of a cultural "other" as the black girls, which would explain their ease in her presence. Even though Pauli is now comfortable with the white girls, she still struggles with her biracial heritage. She cannot wait until she goes to Sarah Lawrence because there is racial diversity there, and she believes: "I'd be happy in a place like that" (Woodson *Maizon* 116). Pauli's statement reveals youthful idealism—that all of her identity problems will be solved once she changes locations. Woodson assumes that her readers will understand that Pauli is not directly confronting her identity issues and, therefore, will continue to struggle with her identity until she does so. "[T]hrough Pauli, Woodson gives voice to the importance of finding one's own way" (Stover 88). By living through Pauli's experiences, young adults learn that they must move beyond naiveté for self-actualization to take place.

Woodson examines the plight of contemporary African American girls and the tightrope they walk trying to be individuals in American society without jeopardizing their ties to the African American collective. In these texts, the writer does not privilege working-class culture. Instead, she reveals that a middle-class and a working-class culture coexist in the African American community. She privileges neither class but encourages her young readers to accept each other despite class differences. Such an approach highlights the diversity in the community and attempts to dispel the notion of ethnic authenticity and social class superiority. Woodson theorizes the complexity of African American ethnic identity in her novels, and in doing so, she has created literature that encourages her young readers to challenge their preconceived notions of social and cultural others. "If the purpose of literature is to liberate, the purpose of [...] multicultural literature is to help liberate us from the preconceived stereotypical hang-ups that imprison us within narrow boundaries" (Howard 92). By constructing and validating new social spaces where African American girls in their works, and in real life, can confidently create positive, strong ethnic and personal identities, Woodson expands the cultural and literary landscape.

3

Loathing the Black Body: Rosa Guy's *The Music of Summer*

Throughout our literary history, African American writers and scholars have openly confronted white cultural oppression and its effects on African American girls and women's lives.[1] It has been known that many scholars try to dispel the western ideology of racialized beauty and femininity that make many black women hate their natural beauty and seek to emulate the Eurocentric standard of beauty. As Robin Tolmach Lakoff and Raquel L. Scherr observe, "[E]urocentric definitions of beauty [...] create feelings of confusion, conflict, self-doubt, and inferiority among those who find their way of looking at the world and at themselves not appreciated" (248). In this chapter, I explore how and why African American women writers of young adult literature continue to discuss the effects of Eurocentric standards of beauty on the self-images of young African American girls—even during the post-Civil Rights/"Black Is Beautiful" era. More specifically, in my analysis of *The Music of Summer* (1992), I study how Rosa Guy portrays Eurocentric standards of beauty as a destructive power that still can corrupt the minds of African American girls, particularly those categorically labeled as middle class.[2]

Feminine beauty in the United States has long been defined by Eurocentric physical characteristics. African American women who possessed light skin and "good hair" were commodities in the marriage market. The preferential treatment that house slaves, frequently mulatto sons and daughters of slave masters, received over the field slaves, who were darker skinned, during slavery contributed to the color hierarchy present in the African American community. Since many mulattos were better prepared to live on their own after emancipation than darker-skinned blacks because of education, money, and land given to them by their white fathers, the economic, hence, social division among the post-slave population continued to grow. To further emphasize the difference, from the late nineteenth century to the mid-twentieth century, the mulatto elite established blue-vein societies that socially separated them from their darker-skinned brethren.[3] The mulatto elite feared association with darker-skinned blacks and aspired to assimilate into the white "race."[4]

Even though the expectation of white acceptance was futile, many light-skinned African Americans continued to go to great lengths throughout the twentieth century to separate themselves from darker-skinned African Americans. With the exception of the "Black Is Beautiful" movement in the 1960s, such preferences for Euro-American standards of beauty has been institutionalized in the African American community.[5] Certain African American churches, sororities, and other social organizations practiced intra-racial discrimination by using assessment methods like the comb test and the paper- bag test to determine the eligibility of members.[6] "Along with light skin tone, blue and green eyes, European shaped noses, and straight as opposed to 'kinky' hair are all accorded higher status both within and beyond the African American community" (Edwards, Carter-Tellison, and Herring 71), which means that outward appearance has economic, personal, political, and social implications for African American woman, especially, in American society. According to Joel Williamson, "[A]s late as 1966 it appeared to some observers that successful darker men were still marrying lighter women. Seemingly, the 'ornamental effect' was still operative. Surveys of high school and college students about the same time also indicated that black was still not generally preferred" (191).[7] Since lighter-skinned African American women historically have been more successful than others in obtaining social and economic strides through marriage, skin color has been a primary factor in determining the quality of life for young African American girls.[8]

Historically, for African Americans as a group this color hierarchy has been closely tied to socio-economics. Quite simply, a higher percentage of the individuals in the African American middle class possess a light complexion. In fact, there has always been an African American middle class in the United States. Albeit small, until recent economic and political advances in the 1960s, the middle class has played a part in the advancement of African Americans. During slavery, some African Americans were free, and they built homes and established businesses under the limited economic and political opportunities. Additionally, some mulatto sons and daughters of slave masters, house slaves, were educated and freed, which gave them more opportunities than the darker-skinned field hands. They often had property and financial support from their fathers. According to Joel Williamson, "wealthy Southern white men were not always willing to alienate forever their darker children from the finer things in life" (23). These African Americans were the beginning of the African American bourgeoisie; the majority of slaves who had these opportunities were therefore of mixed ethnic heritage. Even in the African American community, there developed a correlation between a light skin complexion (a white standard of physical appearance) and economic, moral, and political status.

Consequently, many lighter-skinned blacks discriminated against darker-skinned blacks by barring them from their social clubs, churches, and families. Taken to the extreme, "many very light mulattoes ultimately passed over the color line into whiteness" (Williamson 23). In *The "Hindered Hand": Cultural Implications of Early African-American Fiction*, Arlene Elder argues that many African American novelists even perpetuated the idea that light-skinned African Americans were more noble than darker-skinned African Americans because they wrote for the middle class of both "races" and that publishers expected a negative characterization of dark-skinned African Americans. Elder says social and economic disparities within the African American community also contributed to the negative depictions of lower-class African Americans in nineteenth-century novels. Elder says,

> The distance between the middle-class writers and the masses of their people compounded the problem. After emancipation, the 'house servant/field nigger' division widened within the Black community, one group striving to achieve economic success and social acceptance by acquiring the advantages of higher education and the other, by far the largest number of freedmen, struggling for day by day survival and, at best, literacy. Consequently, an emotional psychological distance developed between the Black masses and the 'talented tenth' who constituted the race's professional class. (33–34).

In *Black Bourgeoisie* (1957), E. Franklin Frazier says that the African American middle class turned its hatred towards whites inward, toward themselves and lower-class African Americans. He says, "[W]hile pretending to be proud of being a Negro [which is the term middle-class African-Americans insisted upon using], they ridicule Negroid physical characteristics and seek to modify or efface them as much as possible. [Their] very use of the term 'nigger,' which they claim to resent, indicates that they want to disassociate themselves from the Negro masses" (226). In her own work, Guy seeks to expose and challenge the color and class hierarchy in the black community; her aim is to improve the lives of all African American girls.

Sarah, the protagonist of *The Music of Summer*, is a talented eighteen-year-old African American pianist who happens to have a dark complexion. She has been friends with Cathy, a blue-eyed, honey-blond-haired, light-skinned African American and main antagonist in the novel, since they were kids. Originally, "They had been key-around-the-neck kids, their mothers working" (6). Their mothers had been both working-class single mothers; Sarah's mother, Lottie, has dark skin while Cathy's mother, Clarice, is light-skinned, blue-eyed, and blond-haired. The dynamic between Sarah and Cathy's mothers is just as important as the dynamic between their daughters because it once again shows that discrimination is learned and that their personal relationship is destroyed by the same intra-racial social and economic politics that ruins their daughters' friendship. The two mothers, Lottie and Clarice, had been close friends during "those Black-Is-Beautiful times of the seventies" (7) when they met at the unemployment office, worked similar jobs, and earned similar salaries. Clarice helped Lottie move into an apartment where she had previously been turned down; this particular apartment housed "light-skinned men and women and black men who handled big money" (8). Theirs was a seemingly strong friendship that was not based on superficial similarities.

However, much has happened since that time. Lottie has become the supervisor of her department, and "Clarice ha[s] found a job in the business she had studied so long and so hard; interior decorating. Things changed, things changed, things changed" (8). Clarice and Cathy have moved to a more exclusive neighborhood and apartment building, and this time Clarice has not helped Lottie gain access into the her building. In a sense, Clarice and Cathy, figuratively and literally, leave Lottie and Sarah behind due to economic and social status based on skin color.

Lottie is bitter toward her former friend and does not want Sarah to associate with either Clarice or Cathy. When she learns that Sarah is planning to visit Cathy at her new apartment, she discourages her. She believes that Cathy and Clarice use Sarah because she is more intelligent than Cathy, and Clarice often asks her to help Cathy prepare for exams. In fact, Clarice often praises Sarah's work ethic while criticizing Cathy. She tells Sarah in front of Cathy, "I must say, Sarah Richardson, you are a good friend. [...] You have the patience of a fool. Even you have to see that Cathy's not serious. I keep spending my money, sending her to good schools, and she just refuses to learn" (22). Sarah reminds Lottie that she and Clarice were best friends—just like she and Cathy are now. Her mother responds, "No, she ain't, Sarah. I'm your best friend. Me! And your aunt Gladys and uncle Sam. Don't go letting those don't give-a-damn high-yeller folks control the lever of your life" (4). Lottie's choice of words indicates she feels that Clarice and Cathy feel and act superior to them because of their skin color. Such "beliefs [have] left many darker-skinned women feeling hostile and resentful toward ... lighter women" (Hunter 72). Hostility can be heard in Lottie's words. She does not want either Cathy or Clarice to influence Sarah's attitudes or behaviors. She furthers her argument by saying, "We dark-skinned Americans always had to keep our eyes on goals. [...] Believe me—what we do, or don't do, depends on us. Life for us is one mighty sea. The waters are damn choppy, so we got to be good swimmers—and that's gospel!" (7). By speaking candidly to Sarah, Lottie is trying to prepare her daughter for the harsh reality of intra- and inter-racial color discrimination. It must also be noted here that when Guy writes that dark-skinned African Americans need to be "good swimmers" to survive the "sea" of societal adversity within and outside of their own ethnic community, the symbolic meaning is not lost on the reader, especially later in the novel when Cathy nearly literally drowns Sarah.

On one hand, this is the type of additional teaching that African American parents must do to prepare their children to cope in an often hostile, racist society that can make their children feel inferior. Lottie is taking on the role of maternal protector. Yet, on the other hand, she may be instilling in Sarah a negative "race" consciousness. By highlighting the plight of dark-skinned African Americans, she is basically teaching Sarah that she must be "two times better" at any activity than her white and light counterparts. In doing so, she seems to be validating the notion that dark-skinned Americans are in a second-class social position in the United States and indirectly instructs Sarah that she is indeed inferior, which undercuts her actual intention to uplift.

To a certain extent this seems to be true because Sarah tries to maintain her relationship with Cathy at the cost of her self-pride and almost her life itself. Sarah says, she and "her mother were alike in one way. They didn't make friends easily" (2), which helps explain why Sarah holds on to the relationship for as long as she does. To cope with Cathy's increasing avoidance and verbal abuse, Sarah forces herself to rely on pleasant memories of friendship with Cathy to soften the blows. As the novel opens, she is wondering why Cathy has not invited her to a tea, a social event which her new light-skinned, upper-middle and upper-class friends have been asked to attend. Cathy offers, "Sarah, I wanted to invite you to—this tea [...] But I know how busy you always are ..." (19). Her feeble excuse is hardly a disguise and facetiously refers to Sarah's dedication to practicing the piano and studying.

It is obvious to the reader and even to Sarah that her friendship with Cathy is waning and that she has purposely not been invited to the tea although she is not ready to acknowledge this. Cathy now believes in her own and her wealthier, light-skinned friends' "superiority" to Sarah due to skin color and socio-economic status. She believes what society, what "every billboard, every movie" (Morrison 39)[9] says about beauty and status; they are cloaked in whiteness and lightness. When Cathy fails to ask Sarah to her family's summer home in Cape Cod, Clarice, invites her despite Cathy's vocal protests.

During summer vacation, Cathy and her friends belittle or ignore Sarah. She is treated as an outsider.[10] However, Cathy's grandmother, Mama Dear, befriends Sarah and makes her feel special—even giving her the special single bedroom Cathy had promised to her new best friend, Sheila. Even the white servant, Alicia, speaks to Sarah. Soon, Mama Dear's worldly and Afro-centric friends, Madame Armand and Jean Pierre, from Martinique come to visit. The son, Jean Pierre, is attracted to Sarah, to her intelligence (She can speak French.) and her "authentic" beauty. At one point, when Cathy tries to flirt with Jean Pierre and to take his attention away from Sarah, he replies "I regret, Cathy. I want so much to hear Sarah play the jazz" (92). Cathy and the other girls are shocked that he would find Sarah more attractive and interesting than they are.

Cathy, in particular, feels bitterness toward Sarah because she is used to all the male attention because of her appearance. She has Milt and Fred, a boy Sarah has actually secretly been attracted to, wrapped around her finger. Cathy may not be a "whiz kid" (121) like Sarah, but she can and has used her appearance to attract boys. "Women [and girls] learn to compete with one another over many traits including educational credentials, income, family status, and perhaps most importantly, beauty. Skin color is closely tied to the definition of beauty such that light-skinned or white women are considered 'more' beautiful than darker-skinned women of color" (Hunter 5).[11] So, when Jean Pierre obviously wants Sarah's attention and not hers, Cathy becomes increasingly angry with Sarah because now Sarah seems to also be treading into the one area, however superficial, in which Cathy has excelled.

Jean Pierre, who becomes Sarah's advocate, protector, and possibly future boyfriend, can see Sarah's beauty. He and his mother, Madame Armand, are from Martinique, a part of the African Diaspora.[12] Jean Pierre has lived in Africa and represents African-inspired culture in the novel. He is a proponent of African standards of beauty; his mind is not clouded by the western beauty aesthetic.

He even explains Cathy's behavior to Sarah. He says that Cathy is jealous and can see that Sarah is actually the more beautiful of the two physically and personality-wise. "She want to see you as ugly. [...] Cathy *wants* to think that you have no right to beauty. But she has good eyes. She can see" (131). In other words, Cathy feels inferior to Sarah, intellectually and physically, so she tries to bolster her own self-esteem by trying to make Sarah feel inferior.

The novel climaxes with Cathy and her friends pitching Sarah into the ocean because they are "playing" with her even though they know she cannot swim. Sarah is only saved from drowning because Jean Pierre appears on the scene. After this experience Sarah is forced to accept that her friendship with Cathy is truly over. The drastic steps that Cathy takes to destroy Sarah and what she represents, blackness, is a bit extreme for young adult literature. However, Guy's effective yet jarring scene illustrates to her young readers the detrimental outcome of self-hatred for African American girls.

William E. Cross, Jr. and Peony Fhagen-Smith write, "[a]s a result of information picked up from inaccurate school texts, television news coverage that overreport Black crime, and historically distorted presentations at museums, and the like, it is fairly easy for *many* Black children to begin to accept as fact information about Black people that is both negative and misleading (miseducation)" (253). Cathy has indeed internalized "negative and misleading" beliefs about black people and blackness itself. Cathy wants Sarah *dead*, not metaphorically or symbolically but literally. Sarah remembers the exact moment she realizes this: "Their eyes met—and spoke, Sarah's saying, *So, Cathy, you wanted me dead.* And the smoky blue eyes narrow with hatred responding with vindictiveness, *I see you didn't die—yet.* Sarah shivered" (157). For Cathy, Sarah is the representation of blackness in general and of Cathy's own blackness, and she wants to eradicate both.

Cathy and her friends' beliefs in their own superiority and their own self-loathing cause them to reach a point where they almost commit a literal homicide and a symbolic genocide,[13] killing blackness. Their hatred of Sarah is truly pathological, and they project it onto Sarah's black body. Betty says, "I never meant to hurt anybody. I don't know what happened. That's the God's truth" (165). What has happened is that she, Cathy, and the others respond violently against their own blackness as represented by Sarah's dark skin. Betty even admits the incident "wasn't just fun and games. Yet we kept going along. I'm so ashamed" (165). Hunter points out that "[c]olorism ... is so bound up in issues of self-esteem and status that sorting out one's perceptions from reality can be very difficult" (108). While fueled by a "mob mentality" and self-hatred, Cathy and her friends move psychologically out of reality and attempt an unspeakable act.

Jody takes over from Betty, continues the story, and says that Cathy had specifically been looking for Sarah. At this point in the novel, Sarah stays to herself. During the beginning of the vacation, she tried to tag along with the others, literally staying on the margins of the group, but they reject her because of her complexion and because her family is working class. At one point, Cathy says, "you're still around like some goddamn dog at my heels. Why don't you go back home and leave us alone! [...] Cathy's hatred seared through Sarah" (122). Fortunately, Sarah does talk to Jean-Pierre, Mama Dear, and Clarice; she is not completely alone during this experience. Also, Lottie's influence helps maintain her sense of self through the summer.

However, when the group does find Sarah, Jody recalls that Milt, a particularly vicious biracial boy who suffers from identity confusion and a hatred of his black father, says, "'Dig that. I don't believe that girl. She's got to be kidding, do you see her in that white bikini?' Then Cathy said, 'What are we waiting for?'" (165). Milt voices his anger at Sarah's "audacity" to wear a white bikini, which actually highlights the darkness of her skin and reveals the shapely curves of her body. In their eyes, especially Cathy and Milt's, Sarah is delighting in the beauty of her darkness, in her growing sensuality, and they despise her for thinking that she is beautiful. They loathe Sarah's black body. It is not surprising then that Milt and Cathy are the main participants in holding Sarah's head underwater. Sarah's ordeal is a terrifying fight for survival.

> Up. Up. A hand on her head! Holding her head! Forcing her down.Down. Down. Desperate. *Hold your breath. Tear at that hand. Rip that hand. Dig fingernails, deep, deep. Get free of that hand. Hold your breath. Fight that hand. Fight. Fight.* Fight a tearing in her chest. Sarah opened her mouth to scream. (153)

Cathy and her friends consider themselves the private Banning High School elite. "They, the Banning school's colored elite, had banded together with nothing in common except that they were middle class and light skinned—an answer to Banning's white students who kept them out of their inner circles. In turn they kept their darker-skinned sisters on the outside looking in" (16). Ultimately, this is an example of the oppressed imitating the oppressors, and Milt's "hand" is the instrument used to hold Sarah down physically (drowning) and psychologically (making her feel inferior). To pacify their own feelings of inferiority in the face of white peers, they seek to make darker-skinned members of their own race feel inferior to them. Cathy and Milt, especially, loathe the black body (black people); their pathology is real and moves them to commit attempted murder.

After the incident, Jean Pierre calls Cathy and her friends, "Criminals! Oui! Cursed children! Sick! Children of diseased souls!" (154). How accurate his words are, especially labeling them "Children of diseased souls." In "Patterns of African American Identity Development: A Life Span Perspective," Cross and Fhagen-Smith say that "learning to place positive or negative value on the color of one's skin (colorism), or feeling either uncomfortable or overly proud about the shape of one's lips, buttocks, or one's hair texture—all examples of lookism—can steer Black children toward a vulnerable self-concept" (253). Arguably, because Cathy suffers from colorism, a disease of the soul, she projects her self-hatred onto Sarah; thereby, trying to instill in Sarah "a vulnerable self-concept" as well.

It must be noted that Guy had Toni Morrison's novel, *The Bluest Eye* (1970), in mind when she wrote *The Music of Summer* because she actually has one character refer to it. Sarah actually reads *The Bluest Eye* in the novel and calls it a "[g]reat book—an American classic. This is my third time reading it" (65). She is reading it while she is alone on the beach; she even offers the book to Alicia, Mama Dear's young white house servant, who is also treated badly by Cathy and her friends because of her perceived lower social class. Sarah is reading because Cathy and the others have excluded her from their activities. Reading is a form of escape for Sarah and also indicates her studious nature. It can be inferred that Sarah can relate to many of the issues raised in the novel, including intra-racial discrimination, especially since she says she has read it three times. This information illustrates the book's importance to Sarah, and subsequently, conveys its importance to young readers. And, more importantly, readers can infer that Guy thinks that this is a significant novel that has connections to her own work; otherwise, she would not have mentioned it in the text. Possibly, they will read Morrison's novel next and continue their love of reading.

More specifically, there are some interesting comparisons between *The Music of Summer* and *The Bluest Eye*. Guy's Cathy, in some ways, is very similar to Morrison's character, Geraldine, a light-skinned, middle-class woman. Geraldine has learned from Eurocentric-based institutions and peers to hate blackness—in skin color, in herself, and what it represents to her, that is, poverty and depravity. She and others like her have attended "land-grant colleges, normal schools, and learn[ed] how to do the white man's work with refinement" (83) and have learned "[t]he careful development of thrift, patience, high morals, and good manners. In short, how to get rid of the funkiness. The dreadful funkiness of passion, the funkiness of nature, the funkiness of the wide range of human emotions" (83). For most scholars, Morrison's "funkiness" is equivalent to "blackness." Morrison illustrates Geraldine's hatred of all things black through her inability to be intimate, to love, or to relate to her black husband or son. Instead, she is dispassionate towards her husband's natural amorous needs and is controlling and selective about her son Junior's lifestyle and playmates—only middle-class African American or white children. To heighten the literary effect and to demonstrate Geraldine's social and psychological alienation due to self-hatred, Morrison has Geraldine only relate to and care about her black cat—a nonhuman. Her disaffected life has reached a disturbing level of social and emotional dysfunction; she suffers from the same "disease" that Cathy does.

Her "disease" also affects and is instilled in Junior, who is well aware that the cat enjoys his mother's affections instead of him. He is growing up to be an alienated and cruel young man; his mother is teaching him well. For example, he invites Pecola into their home on the pretense of befriending her. She begins playing with the cat and out of jealousy and knowledge of his mother's love for the cat, he kills it. When Geraldine enters, he pins the death on Pecola, and Geraldine's response clearly illustrates her hatred of blackness. When she says, "get out [...] you nasty little black bitch. Get out of my house" (92), Geraldine is trying to erase blackness from her sight, to remove blackness from her house. After all, Pecola and her "dirty torn dress" (91) represent *all* of the poor, under-class African Americans in Geraldine's eyes. "She had seen this little girl all of her life. [...] They sat in little rows on street curbs, crowded into pews at church taking space from the nice, neat, colored children" (91–92). Although Geraldine does not literally try to kill Pecola, her actions contribute to the madness and later psychological death of Pecola at the end of the novel. Yet another adult "teaches" Pecola that she is worthless and that her worthlessness is directly connected to her dark complexion.

Oftentimes, prejudice—whether inter- or intra-racial—is a learned behavior. "[P]readolescence [and adolescence] may show the early signs of a youthful but damaged self-concept that reflects in part the internalized racism ... found among the belief systems of their parents or significant others" (Cross and Fhagen-Smith 253). Yes, Cathy learned about the value of her skin color and physical features from society, but she also learned it from her mother. (Interestingly, it can be noted that in *The Bluest Eye*, Geraldine also passes on to Junior hatred of blackness in himself and in others.) Although Clarice does not intentionally try to teach Cathy intra-racial discrimination, her actions do. At the end of the novel, Sarah confronts Clarice asking her to confirm or deny something that Cathy has told her: "Cathy told me that I ought to be more like my mother and stop going where I wasn't wanted" (168). Clarice admits that she did ask Lottie not to come to see her at her job anymore because of her boss. She explains, "I couldn't afford to lose my job. So I told Lottie to cool it, that I'd see her back at my apartment" (169). Clarice goes further and lets everyone know that she has "passed" for white to acquire the job and improve her financial situation. "With all the hoopla of what a great city we live in, we all know that there are places blacks can't go. I wouldn't have been hired if my boss had known that I was black" (169). The truth is revealed; Clarice not only has denied her friend but also her black identity for material gain. Sarah now knows the depths of her mothers' pain and anger and why she no longer associates with Clarice. "Suddenly Sarah understood: Shame. Lottie's shame expressed itself as rage!" (169).

Although Cathy's behavior is also connected to her envy of Sarah's intelligence and talent, she is also using parental modeling to justify her behavior toward Sarah. She is only acting like her mother did to her former best friend, rejecting her for a perceived better life. She learns to hate blackness and to act cruelly just like Junior in *The Bluest Eye*. In other words, in Cathy's "sick" mind, her mother's rejection of Lottie validates/justifies Cathy's rejection of Sarah despite her mother's words of acceptance and friendship. Immediately after her confession, Clarice is embarrassed and recognizes her role in her daughter's attitudes and actions. Mama Dear says, "An unhappy mistake. Problem is, it ain't ours—never ours—to decide. Yet it's us what got to be responsible. Whatever happen, we got to keep loving one another. Got to examine things and talk them out—or these mistakes we making today spills over from one generation to the next—getting thicker and thicker with each new layer…" (170). Through Mama Dear's words, Guy is commenting on how inter- and intra-racial discrimination is passed down from one generation to another. Yes, it may have started because of white racism, but it is the responsibility of those in the African American community to acknowledge its existence and to heal it. She wants young readers to recognize this fact, to become aware of prejudice—intra- and inter-racial—in their own lives and to try to eliminate it. "By uncovering the beauty queue and debating the high status of white [or light] beauty, we expose white racism and female objectification" (Hunter 121). Whereas their parents' and/or grandparents' generations started this debate in the 1960s, Guy encourages young readers to continue the debate and to oppose inter- and intra-racial discrimination.

Despite her torment, Sarah remains a compassionate person. She hopes that "[p]erhaps as Cathy grew old, lonely, and friendless, she might be able to see through the fog of her rage and to determine the enemy—and use her anger *for* friends instead of against them" (173). Sarah rightly recognizes that Cathy's self-hatred and delusion prevent her from understanding that the "enemy" is the society that has taught her that blackness is inferior to whiteness and lightness. She also realizes that if Cathy can ever conquer the delusion, she would be able to use righteous anger against the society to encourage social change, and to ultimately, help her friends overcome societal oppression instead of being a part of the oppression of her friends.

At the end of *The Music of Summer*,[14] Guy leaves Sarah in Jean Pierre's embrace, the embrace of cultural acceptance, love, and support. Sarah has survived Cathy's worst efforts to destroy her and is now stronger. Jean Pierre tells Sarah about Africa and how "it is Africa who sold you out. Do you know many of our people were sold in slavery by jealous kings? Our great thinkers, musicians, our warriors. ... We cannot help being a great people" (113). While Jean Pierre maintains a balanced view of Africa, acknowledging Africans' role in the African slave trade, he also speaks of its greatness and the greatness of its people in the African Diaspora. In doing so, he is instilling in Sarah a stronger sense of self and cultural identity. "All you have to guard against here [in the United States] is that they [those who discriminate whether white or black] do not kill the spirit. You have brought the soul here, to stay for eternity. The spirit—it must survive" (113), and it does in Sarah's tenacity and willingness to survive all of life's trials. She will not be like Pecola who falls into madness after her spirit is crushed and experiences psychological death at the end of *The Bluest Eye*. For Sarah, this "spirit" is "the music of summer," learning how to survive all of life's trials, the ups and downs, over the course of the summer. Her "spirit" helps her survive and abandon a dangerous relationship with Cathy and embrace a new nurturing one with Jean Pierre. Guy hopes that that same "spirit" will be instilled in her young readers as well so that like Sarah, young African American girls will have the wherewithal to not only survive but thrive in the world despite personal and "racial" turmoil and strife.

4

The African American Vernacular Tradition and Sexual Identity in Jacqueline Woodson's *The House You Pass on the Way*

The African American Vernacular Tradition,[1] whether Negro spirituals, folktales, or "signifyin," illustrates and has illustrated African Americans' cleverness, emotional strength, individuality, and inventiveness over the years. In Jacqueline Woodson's *The House You Pass on the Way* (1997), Staggerlee, the female protagonist, chooses to name herself after a legendary "bad" man in the African American vernacular tradition because her burgeoning sexual preference makes her feel like an outsider, a rebel, much like the folk hero. By identifying with Staggerlee, the protagonist, gains emotional and psychological validation from her cultural heritage. As a result, she is empowered and feels secure enough to embrace her sexual orientation.

The public often believes that the purpose of children's and young adult literature is to provide moral instruction and to entertain. These are old yet enduring notions. Teachers customarily use such literature as a tool to hone students' literary skills, preparing them to graduate to adult literature. In the contemporary academic scene and in the consumer marketplace, children's and young adult literature is still viewed as an educational tool but also as a way to "help children grapple with their personal problems and become aware of social concerns" (Rudman 2). Contemporary writers of children's and young adult literature such as Woodson have continued to build on the groundbreaking work of past writers and to hold to the educational and entertainment elements of the literature, but they also continue to push the boundaries of literary content. As a result, public perceptions and those of critics of young adult literature began to change during the mid-1960s when more controversial topics like child abuse, divorce, and sexual orientation began appearing in works. Some of the other newer issues are cross-cultural adoptions, mental illness, and street life for runaways. Contemporary writers are able to more openly and directly address these issues.

Young adult literature, even children's literature, is no longer viewed as a realm of innocence: "[T]he violence and neglect that many children [and young adults] experience on a daily basis have become a permanent part of children's literature" (Lehr xiii).[2] However, writers of young adult literature, past and present, have had to contend with censorship. Every year, articles appear in local newspapers telling stories about concerned school boards and/or parents, who are trying to remove certain books such as Mark Twain's *Huckleberry Finn* (1855) and Maya Angelou's *I Know Why the Caged Bird Sings* (1971) from primary and secondary school reading lists because they contain "objectionable" language or content. Judy Blume, a well-known writer of young adult fiction, has faced censorship often during her career. In the introduction to *Places I Never Meant to Be: Original Stories by Censored Writers*, she says, "[T]his obsession with banning books continues as we approach the year 2000. Today it is not only Sex, Swear Words and Lack of Moral Tone—it is Evil, which, according to the censors, can be found lurking everywhere. […] [T]here's not an *ism* you can think of that's not bringing some book to the battlefield" (8).

Places I Never Meant to Be is a collection of stories by writers who have been censored, Woodson included. While commenting on censorship, Woodson remembers, "[O]nce I received a stack of letters from sixth-graders telling me why I shouldn't write a certain book they heard (from their teachers) was being published. Once an illustrator refused to illustrate the cover of a novel of mine because she found it 'offensive'" (82). Even though she has received criticism, Woodson continues to write about topics that interest her as a writer and that she believes are important for young people:

> [A]s a child and young adult, I wrote for myself, to get a better sense of the world around me, to be happy. I have gone back to that beginning […] and have once again found my solace in the writing. Like the censorship, like racism and homophobia and all the other hatreds in the world, the writing, too, will always be here—giving me a better sense of the world around me, helping me to grow and understand. (82)

Because Woodson has decided not to bow to the whims of censors, her young readership also gains a better sense of the world around them by reading her thought-provoking fictionalized portrayals of their lives.

Young adult novels are written for an audience that is meant to identify with the protagonist and his/her problems. I believe the writer's concern with reader/character identification is one of the main reasons that many (certainly not all) young adult novels are written with contemporary characters, social issues, and settings. Woodson is a wonderful example of a writer who is very concerned with creating characters that her audience can recognize. When Woodson says, "I want to open up a book and see myself in it and by extension, not feel isolated in the world. I believe it's important for young people to have this," she is explaining that she wants her audience to be able to recognize themselves in her characters and settings. As a result, her readers may also find solutions to similar problems and concerns.

In *The House You Pass on the Way*, Woodson is advocating for a more tolerant view of lesbianism and trying to foster sexual tolerance in her readers at a young age.[3] Such an attempt is controversial, especially for young readers. However, since discrimination is taught to children at a young age,[4] it is important to begin teaching tolerance as soon as possible to counter the negative effects of ethnic and sexual bias. Additionally, Woodson is challenging the African American community to acknowledge the presence of homosexuality among their own for "non-heterosexuality is especially strongly maligned among some people of color" (Perrin 14). While sexuality issues have appeared in young adult literature since the 1960s, the earlier writers addressed the issue indirectly by including a homosexual minor character or by tragically depicting a homosexual protagonist. In doing so, they minimized the significance of recognizing and understanding sexual orientation for their young readers. Woodson, however, addresses sexual orientation directly. In *The House You Pass on the Way*, she pushes the limits of acceptable content in African American young adult literature.[5]

Because of her sexuality, Staggerlee has not been able to establish lasting peer relationships unlike her older siblings, who are socially active. Instead, to a certain extent, she feels isolated from her family and others because of her sexual orientation. When Staggerlee earnestly expresses her desire for Trout to visit, she wonders, "[W]as it that obvious [to her parents] [...] how lonely she was?" (21).[6] She feels isolated because of her homosexual feelings and does not believe she can confide in her family because of their negative attitudes about homosexuals. "Homosexuality is a stigmatizing characteristic that is not generally shared by other members of the family. Race, national/ethnic heritage, religion, even socioeconomic status are shared within the family. Children may grow up knowing that they are discredited in the wider society, but they feel sure of the support of the family. Not so with homosexuality" (Perrin 16).

Staggerlee's isolation is also illustrated by the title of the novel, *The House You Pass on the Way*. When a traveler passes a house as he drives along a highway, all he can see is a façade—wood, brick, or vinyl siding. However, unless she passes an occasional open window, the traveler is not able to determine what events are taking place inside the house. Likewise, an outside observer would not know about the turmoil Staggerlee feels just by looking at her. She conceals her feelings out of fear and to a certain extent shame. Staggerlee feels alienated from family and peers because of her sexual orientation; like a house on a highway, people pass by her, rarely stopping to engage her. Staggerlee's fourteen-year-old cousin, Trout, experiences many of the same feelings.

Trout is the adopted daughter of Ida Mae, Staggerlee's father's estranged sister, and her husband, Jonathan. Her father and his family have not spoken in years because his sisters did not approve of his marriage to a white woman. Consequently, Staggerlee "had never met Ida Mae—only knew of her from the stories her father told" (10). However, the death of their sister, Hallique, encourages Ida Mae to reach out to her brother: "[Jonathan] and I got to talking and we figured all these years of having family all disconnected have just been a waste of good living" (17–18). However, her desire for family reconciliation is only one reason Trout is sent to visit Staggerlee and her family.

On her deathbed, Hallique told Ida to be patient with Trout because she was having homosexual feelings and had kissed a girl; "Ida lost it" (70). In Ida Mae's mind, Trout may lose her desire for girls if she leaves Baltimore for a while. Obviously, Trout has been closer to Hallique than to Ida Mae because she confided in her. She remembers that Hallique allayed her sexual anxiety by telling her, "I'd get crushes on lots of people, boys and girls" (75). It has been important for Trout that an adult took her confusion seriously and listened to her, thereby, validating her feelings. Even so, Hallique also told her that if she continues to have these feelings she should not tell anyone, so while Hallique validates Trout's temporary sexual confusion, she implies that choosing to be a lesbian, is wrong. As a result, it is not surprising that Trout begins dating a boy after she returns home.

Months later in a letter to Staggerlee, she reveals that she didn't know how to tell her that she liked a boy. After sharing their secret sexual orientation, Trout does not want Staggerlee to feel abandoned by her: "I want us to be like we were last summer, close like that, even if we don't have the girl thing in common anymore" (96). To a certain extent, Staggerlee does feel deserted by Trout; she believes she has given in to pressure from Ida Mae and her best friend, Rachel. Woodson comments, "Staggerlee knows who she is for the most part, but her friend Trout is struggling, conforming, trying to fit in somewhere" (968). However, at this point in their lives, sexual confusion is not uncommon and can lead to sexual experimentation. Perrin says, that during adolescence, "the development of an adult understanding of and attitude toward sexuality is in flux" (71). The novel ends with Staggerlee's thoughts: "[T]hey were both waiting. Waiting for this moment, this season, these years to pass. Who would they become? She wondered. Who would they become?" (99).[7]

Even though Staggerlee finds validation for her homosexual feelings by sharing her trepidation with Trout, she is aware of her sexual confusion well before Trout enters her life. Hazel, her former best friend, is also the first girl whom she has kissed. When Hazel rejects Staggerlee because other black girls convince her that she is conceited, Staggerlee is hurt because of class jealousy and ethnic bias but also because she loses the first girl she expresses love for.[8] "Hazel succumbs to peer pressure, and turns away from Staggerlee, leaving her all the more alone" (Stover 121).

In *Sexual Orientation in Child and Adolescent Health Care*, Ellen C. Perrin acknowledges that homosexuality is generally stigmatized in most cultures, and because of societies' response to "non-heterosexuality," "it serves to marginalize people who are gay or lesbian, limits their opportunities and their social networks, and threatens their self-esteem" (15). Hazel's disdain reinforces Staggerlee's belief that something is wrong with having romantic feelings for girls. In fact, "Staggerlee recalls how she had felt the afternoon after she had kissed Hazel, how she had started running home, aching to tell someone, but how she slowed down, knowing nobody at home would want to celebrate with her" (Stover 123). Later in the novel, she explains her anxiety to Trout: "[N]o one ever told me I had to lie about it or had to keep it quiet, but somehow I just knew. [...] I have all this stuff—all these thoughts going on inside me and they all seem so—so dangerous" (81). Being able to talk honestly with Trout about her sexuality and identifying with Trout's experiences enable Staggerlee to understand those thoughts that seem so dangerous. She knows that society does not accept homosexuality, and therefore, she "just knew" that she should openly discuss her sexuality only with those who feel the same way she does or not at all.[9]

Staggerlee makes an astute comparison between her mother's reaction to menstruation and her mother's hypothetical reaction to a lesbian daughter. She remembers that when she began her menstrual cycle her mother "had given her a taste of wine for becoming a woman" (69). She celebrated, but Staggerlee believes that her mother's reaction would be different if she knew how she felt about girls: "[She and Trout] were alone together. There was no one standing behind a closed door smiling and holding out a glass of wine" (70) in celebration. Staggerlee's dream of being isolated in the snow further reveals her anxiety about her sexuality.

Unlike Trout, who benefits from an adult telling her that it is okay to be attracted to both sexes, Staggerlee keeps her secret hidden and only reveals it to Trout. Identifying with Trout and developing a friendship with her over the summer is enough to build her confidence and to encourage her to see her sexual orientation as normal; she even becomes more social and makes new friends. Her bildungsroman journey has begun; she is learning that she will have to oppose society's, and possibly her family's, aversion to homosexuality to embrace her sexual identity.

At the end of the novel when she asks herself, "Who would they become?" (99), Staggerlee is wondering about her life and Trout's in general but also whether they will be heterosexual or homosexual. While Trout seems to be leaning toward heterosexuality because of her new and enjoyable relationship with Matthew, Staggerlee seems to be leaning toward homosexuality because she has consistently preferred girls. Even so, the fact that Staggerlee asks herself the question suggests that her sexual orientation will be continually revealed as she goes through the maturation process. "The reader hopes that Staggerlee, too, will grow into an awareness of the complexities of herself, of how 'gay' does not describe all of who she is and can be" (Stover 124–25), and "Woodson [gives] both [Trout] and Staggerlee space, through their separation, to just 'be'" (Stover 126).

It is also interesting to note that the two main characters use names they have chosen for themselves. "The girls are alike in their search for identity, in their renaming of themselves" (Stover 122). Staggerlee's real name is Evangeline, but now "her name, Staggerlee, [...] was her own. A name she had given herself a long, long time ago" (3). Trout's real name is the androgynous Tyler: "Ida and Jonathan tried that name out on me" (47). However, when she arrives, she tells the family, "[M]y name is Trout" (46). She even says that her birth mother gave her yet another name, Danielle. Self-naming is, obviously, an attempt to define oneself and create one's own identity.

Staggerlee takes her name from a song her grandfather sang as part of his vaudeville act. Interestingly, she chooses a name that is infamous in the African American vernacular tradition. Lawrence Levine says, "[T]he legendary prototype for many of these figures [bad men/notorious folk heroes], the most important and longest-lived bad man in black lore, was Stagolee, who was known also as Stackolee, Stackerlee, Stackalee, Stacker Lee, and Staggerlee" (413).[10]

In the story, Woodson even offers a version of the Staggerlee legend when the family watches their grandfather's performance of the song on videotape:

> [H]e ain't had no limits, that ole boy, Staggerlee,/Put him in a prison box, he'd find the key or/Break the lock/Couldn't keep him locked inside, that old boy,/ Staggerlee. [...] Staggerlee went to Heaven but Heaven's gate/was closed/St. Peter told him, men like you be better off/down below/Staggerlee went on down there, but the Devil/turned his back/Staggerlee said, "There ain't no right or wrong./There ain't no white or black [...]." (27, 29)

Young Staggerlee interprets the verses to mean that Staggerlee, the legend, has freed himself from society's restrictions and recognizes no limitations on his life choices—whether they are viewed by society as "good" or "bad." She incorporates that understanding into her own life and realizes that if she becomes a lesbian she, too, will have to oppose social convention. Jerry H. Bryant posits that "[o]utlaws ... Can be a source of nourishment and liberation for the African American community, leading the more timid into new modes of consciousness, toward otherwise inconceivable choices and identities" (180), and it is clear that the Staggerlee legend is functioning in this way for Staggerlee, the protagonist.[11]

Woodson wants her character to feel strong, secure, and empowered, so the young girl takes the name of this particular "bad man." However, in her grandfather's version, Staggerlee, the legend, is more of a hero than a "bad man," and young Staggerlee can hear "the story inside the story" (Woodson 28), the heroic character elements. Her grandfather sings, "[H]e ain't had no limits, that ole boy, Staggerlee,/ Put him in a prison box, he'd find the key or/break that lock/Couldn't keep him locked inside, the old boy, Staggerlee" (27–28). Staggerlee knows that Staggerlee, the legend, is supposed to have "shot a man for a five-dollar hat and went on to be known as the most evil man alive" (28).

In the last stanza, Staggerlee learns that she will have to develop her own beliefs to successfully achieve her true identity. When Staggerlee, the legend, says, "[T]here ain't no right or wrong./There ain't no white or black," (29) Staggerlee is encouraged to see her sexual orientation as normal, not subject to society's judgment. Also, she feels less anxious about her biracial heritage because Staggerlee, the legend, minimizes ethnic differences as well. Woodson skillfully uses the Staggerlee legend to symbolically illustrate her protagonist's life struggles and triumphs.

By choosing the name of a man her grandfather admired, Staggerlee strengthens her ties to her family, takes pride in her grandparents' contributions in the civil rights movement, and creates for herself a sense of cultural identity, family, and, therefore, belonging. Now, as an adolescent, her name gives her strength to express her sexuality. Because of her homosexual feelings, she feels like she must "break out of the gates of life" (28) that cause her to think that she needs to hide her sexual orientation. She once again needs Staggerlee's strength to help her establish her sexual identity. It is also important to mention here that Woodson has Staggerlee identify with a masculine hero. Consequently, her self-selected masculine name possibly further illustrates her lack of attraction to the "opposite" sex.

Although Woodson in a personal interview says that she chose the name "Trout" for the character because "I just like the name," I see a symbolic relationship with her character. Trout renames herself because she is trying to create an identity. She is an adopted child who needs a sense of belonging. Her relationship with her parents seems distant. She is wrestling with her homosexual feelings and fears that they are abnormal and cannot confide in her parents, for example. By self-naming, Trout seeks a linguistic place of belonging. In fact, "Trout changed her name after watching a trout fight its way upstream, [...] and Trout feels like she has to fight constantly" (Stover 122). By taking on a name like Trout, she might hope that she will develop a self-sufficiency and inner strength that will lead to freedom. Renaming herself enables Trout to begin living her life on her own terms and to begin to express her own desires. Additionally, the name, Trout, is not necessarily gender specific. As a result, Trout is further distancing herself from society's constricting gender boundaries.

Woodson's in-depth depiction of girls coming to terms with their sexuality is a bold move for a writer of African American young adult literature, even in contemporary times. Even after being criticized and censored for earlier works like *The Dear One* (1991) and *I Hadn't Meant to Tell You This* (1994), she continues to tackle the difficult subjects like sexual orientation. In a personal interview, she says, "I think it's important that young people see the diversity of cultures and classes" (Woodson) and because she depicts her homosexual characters with compassion, I believe that she also wishes young people to accept others' alternative lifestyles. By reading about issues of sexual orientation, young girls may feel comfortable talking about their own struggles with sexuality—heterosexual and homosexual: "[A]lthough it is more difficult for children to locate and acquire these books than to obtain those in any other category, children often manage to share what they do find with each other. Peer education and malediction on this topic are greater than on any other. [...] Books can help [them find the correct information]" (Rudman 5–6). Woodson's novel is an effective way to begin this often-silenced discussion.

5

Inter-racial Friend/Relationships in Jacqueline Woodson's *I Hadn't Meant to Tell You This* and *Lena* and Virginia Hamilton's *A White Romance*

Inter-racial friendships and relationships are not often explored in African American young adult literature. It is an issue that uncomfortably forces most people—adults as well as children—to directly address racism and discrimination. At times, the individuals in the relationship will have to address their own personal biases toward inter-racial friendships and/or relationships. Other times, the individuals involved have to contend with how those outside of the relationship respond to their personal choices to be involved in an inter-racial friendship/relationship. One of the main reasons that people who try to foster inter-racial friendships/relationships may experience problems is the issue of trust. Trust is an important factor in the development of all deep friendships and relationship. In Rebecca Carroll's *Sugar in the Raw: Voices of Young Black Girls in America*, Tiffany, a young African American girl states, "I have close white girlfriends at school. They're close, but not *real* close. There is a fine line between close and real close, but I guess what it really comes down to is trust. [...] With my white friends, I don't think about being close or real close, I just know that there is a difference between being close and real close" (138).[1]

Because of the historical (and current) practice of "racial" discrimination, the United States has been, and arguably continues to be, a nation divided along racial and ethnic lines. As a result, persons of differing ethnicities have difficulty trusting each other, and because trust is a key element in the development of social relationships, inter-racial friendships and romantic relationships can be difficult to forge, especially at an early age since kids generally have to follow adult guidelines and not their own. In this chapter, I study Jacqueline Woodson's *I Hadn't Meant to Tell You This* (1994) and *Lena* (1999) and Virginia Hamilton's novel, *A White Romance* (1987) to explain how difficulties such as adult prejudice and peer pressure interfere with young adults who choose to cross designated ethnic boundaries.

In *I Hadn't Meant to Tell You This* and *Lena*, characters directly talk about how racism affects their relationships. By having her characters confront this issue in their dialogue, Woodson stresses her belief that friendships among girls are difficult to create and that societal problems do influence them. In an interview, she says, "[T]rue friendship is complex and rewarding and difficult. Everyone knows that. Young people truly know that. [...] The novels talk about friendship but they [are] talking about bigger themes in talking about friendship—race, class, sexuality, family, etc." Additionally, Woodson directly explains why she discussed inter-racial friendship in these two novels in a statement for Random House Publishers: "I really wanted to write about friendship. I wanted to write about people crossing racial lines to be friends and people crossing class line" (qtd. in Stover 65).[2]

In *I Hadn't Meant to Tell You This*, Woodson creates an intriguing story about child abuse, racism, and classism by using two characters, Marie, middle class and black, and Lena, working class and white. In fact, a number of Woodson's novels depict relationships between black and white girls and the difficulties they have in forging real and lasting friendships.[3] Marie in *I Hadn't Meant to Tell You This* has to confront her own and her father's suspicion of whites and peer prejudice before developing a friendship with Lena. However, Marie is able to overcome prejudice and create a real relationship with Lena as exhibited when Lena entrusts her with a secret that she has shared with no one else, that her father sexually abuses her.

The story is set in Chauncey, a black suburb of Athens, Ohio, where blacks are overwhelmingly middle class and whites are working class and live "across the railroad tracks," a "classic" class demarcation line. At Chauncey's Middle and High schools, "[the white kids] don't stay long, and it's rare you see black kids hanging out with them. [...] They keep to themselves, bring their lunches in grease-stained brown paper bags, eat huddled around the tables in the farthest corners of the cafeteria, their heads bowed in silence" (*Hadn't Meant* 4). Woodson's Marie is well aware of the socio-economic differences between black and white kids in Chauncey and knows that she has a higher economic status than neighboring whites. Further, bolstered by her father's prejudice, especially against poor whites, whom he calls, "[T]rash," (5), she also believes she has a higher social status.

In this unique social environment, then, Marie is not in close contact with white girls because of class differences as well as ethnic ones. In school, she says, "I never really talked to any of the white kids at Chauncey before" (29). When Lena enrolls in school, Marie is assigned to be Lena's class escort. Marie and her best friend, Sherry, are less than thrilled. During lunch, Sherry calls Lena white trash and encourages Marie to stop escorting Lena to her classes. When Marie, who is starting to feel sorry for Lena, refuses to take her advice, "Sherry sucked her teeth. 'You're just being an Uncle Tom.'"[4] As Marie and Lena's friendship grows, Marie and Sherry's relationship withers.

After Sherry accuses Marie of kissing up to Lena, Marie realizes that she has been too influenced by Sherry: "[S]o many girls at Chauncey wanted to be like Sherry, myself included. If it hadn't been for Sherry, I wouldn't have been voted Best Dressed. I mimicked her style and added my own touches only when I realized I could *dress* myself and look halfway decent" (36). While she is not completely ready to let go of her relationship with Sherry, Marie begins the painful process of becoming her own person and making her own choices. Near the end of the novel, it is Sherry who initiates a reconciliation.

In a last ditch effort to bring Marie back into her group, Sherry asks her if she will be socializing with Lena. Marie, who is at this point still trying to decide, says, "I'm not going to be hanging with her much. [...] [P]robably just today and that's it. You know I don't really care for white people. [...] Especially white trash" (51). By calling Lena a demeaning name, Marie performs as she believes Sherry wants her to. She even looks over at Lena before saying the name, stressing her intent and strengthening its meaning for Sherry. She performs this move to assuage Sherry's fears that she is trying to leave her Black peers for a white one. Marie, like many adolescents, is concerned with how she is perceived by her peer group and seeks social groupings where she fits. Such groups, as in this case, are often based on ethnicity. Eventually though, Marie learns to overlook ethnic differences and realizes that she and Lena have more in common, especially their absent mothers, than she does with Sherry. Lena's mother has died of cancer, and Marie's mother has left the family in search of a life for herself, separate from her family.[5]

Moreover, Marie has to ignore, even challenge, her father's prejudice against whites to establish a relationship with Lena. When Marie tells her father about

Lena for the first time, he cautions her, "I don't know if you should think about her too much. They come here for a little while, then they're off to the next place" (29). As the girls' friendship grows, Lena and her younger sister, Dion, start visiting her home. Her father, who refers to Lena and Dion as "those girls" says, "[B]ut I don't like the looks of those girls. I don't like their clothes, their eyes—" (67), disguising his bigotry. Beverly Daniel Tatum believes that "Adults, both White and of color, often hesitate to speak [directly] to children about racism for fear they will create problems where perhaps none exist, afraid that they will make 'colorblind' children unnecessarily color-conscious" (xvi). This is partially the case for Marie's father initially; however, his own bias soon becomes more obvious to Marie. Marie's father wants her to reestablish ties with Sherry. Marie, however, is perceptive and directly challenges her father's prejudice, telling him that "you're stuck in the sixties. This is the nineties" (*Hadn't Meant* 69), and getting him to admit to her that he doesn't like them because they are white.

This time is not the first Marie has challenged her father's views. Earlier in the novel, she asks her father to explain the difference between the use of the words "nigger" and "white trash," the word she heard Sherry use in the cafeteria. After explaining that nigger has more linguistic power because whites oppress blacks and that "[*W*]*hitetrash* is just easier" (28) to say because it gives blacks linguistic power to retaliate against whites, he says, "None of it's right. Just how the world is. White people hate us, and we go on hating them right back" (28). Marie gives a perceptive response: "I would think white trash [the group] is just as disenfranchised as black people" (28). In an impressive move toward maturation, Marie is able to empathize with the economic plight of poor whites.[6] The girl who once had never spoken to a white girl now defends her relationship with Lena and tells her father, "I trust her, Daddy. She's different" (69). The ability to judge the values one's parents teach and to accept or reject them is part of the maturation process present in a coming-of-age journey. Marie has begun the process.

Lena also has to defy her father's prejudice to befriend Marie. In one of the girls' first frank discussions, Lena admits that her father, "[C]alls this a nigger school. Say I'm a nigger lover 'cause I had this friend, you know. We was real tight, and she was a black girl. He don't really like mixing races. Sometimes I try to argue with him, tell him this is the nineties and all. But he say if God wanted us to mix, he would've made us all one color" (40–41).

Because Marie's father discourages her relationship with Lena, it is ironic that Lena begins revealing her own father's abuse by asking Marie, "[Y]our daddy [...] is he [...] nice" (39) and telling her that she could not love her own father. Eventually, Lena tells Marie about her abuse, but Woodson does not use the graphic violence and language that is present in adult literature. She is conscious of her young readership.

Instead, mindful of her audience, Woodson has Lena tell Marie subtly: "I bet you can be in your house naked. [...] I bet you can lock your bathroom door. I bet you can stand in front of your mirror every morning and take a good long look at yourself without [...] without anything happening to you" (54) and "[Y]our daddy never touches you like the way ..." (55). Lena even cuts her hair short and never washes it so that she will be less appealing to her father.[7] Even though Woodson is subtle, young readers and Marie can understand Lena's meaning: "I knew what Lena was getting at. I had read about stuff like this. But it couldn't happen to anybody I knew. It happened to sad, foreign girls in Third World countries. To girls living in crowded apartments. Or in the South. What was it doing here, in Chauncey, Ohio?" (54). Marie does not want to believe Lena and even calls her a liar because "[N]o father is like that" (55). Eventually, however, Marie does believe Lena. And, when Lena tells her that she plans to run away from home because "he's touching Dion now" (111), Marie tries to convince Lena to tell the authorities about the abuse, instead of running away.

At the end of the novel, when she tells Marie her plan, Marie wants to tell the authorities, but Lena makes her promise not to tell anyone. In *Lena*, the sequel to *I Hadn't Meant to Tell You This*, Woodson details Lena and Dion's lives as runaways. She and Dion are hitchhiking to Pine Mountain in Kentucky, hoping their mother's relatives will take them in despite the fact that these family members never sought to take them after their mother passed away. Even so, Lena tries to keep her spirits high by remembering her mother. She seeks safety and security in her mother's memory. By the end of this novel, Lena and Dion learn that Marie has revealed Lena's secret to her father and that he has been searching for them.

While staying with Miz Lily, a kindly African American woman who picks them up as hitchhikers and takes them in, Lena finally reaches out to her "best friend" (*Lena* 4) through a telephone call. When Marie answers, she calls out Sherry's name, and Lena immediately thinks that Marie has replaced her and has reestablished her "best" friendship with Sherry. Lena soon realizes that this is not the case. Marie quickly recognizes that it is Lena and tells her "Everybody's looking for you, Lena! My father called all these people. We thought—I was afraid" (85). After Marie's father discusses the situation with authorities and Miz Lily, he arranges for them to fly back to Chauncey and agrees to let them stay with his family. Marie tells Lena, "He's different now. Now that I told him everything— [...] He really wants to find you and Dion. He told me he wants everything to turn out all right" (89). In this situation, a child has influenced the belief system and attitudes of an adult, as indicated by Marie's father's newfound compassion for two white girls. Lena also learns from Marie that her own father has left town, which relieves her, and seems to imply that he will never return to actively abuse her or Dion although Lena may have to undergo psychological treatment in the near future to help her cope with the previous abuse. The novel ends with a tired, yet hopeful, Lena returning to Chauncey. She is now being provided a real, not imagined "home," with an African American family. She confidently tells a fellow airplane passenger that she and Dion are "heading home" (115). No doubt this "mixed" family will face some intra- and inter-racial prejudice in Chauncey; however, each of these characters has individually faced and conquered their own prejudices. It therefore can be inferred that they will be able to overcome the negative influences of outside forces.

Additionally, while we know child abuse does not occur only in poor families, it is interesting to note that Lena is poor and suffers academically in school because of the abuse: "[O]ne week Lena would ace her math quiz, the following week she'd get a D on a social studies paper" (*Hadn't Meant* 94). By the end of *I Hadn't Meant to Tell You This*, Lena has developed a close relationship with Marie, but Lena has not developed trusting relationships with adults who could contact social services to bring about change in her life. This mentoring must wait for the sequel, *Lena* (1999). While on the road, Lena and Dion are fortunate enough to find adults who do not take advantage of them but provide them with transportation, food, and sometimes money. However, it is the relationship that Lena, in particular develops with Miz Lily that further bolsters her and Dion's ability to trust and establish relationships across ethnic borders and continues to encourage them to trust adults.

When Miz Lily gives the girls a ride, Dion is initially hesitant; Lena says that they have not accepted a ride from a black person on their journey, "[n]ot because we didn't want them, just 'cause nobody was offering" (*Lena* 56). However, Lena knows that Dion's hesitation is due to their father's prejudice towards black people. She says: "Dion's face scrunched up a bit, the way Daddy's used to when he saw black people. I felt heat rise up to my head and had to put my hand in my pocket to keep from decking her with it" (57). While Lena has been able to completely overcome her father's negative influence, the younger Dion is still in the process of unlearning racist attitudes. Lena is and will continue to be a role model for Dion through her interactions with people across ethnic boundaries. As they ride and talk, Lena tells Miz Lily the same story, she and Dion are traveling to meet their mother at a nearby hospital, that they have told all interested adults they've met while on their journey. However, Miz Lily can sense that the girls' story is false even though she does not let them know until later. Instead, once she realizes that no one is there to meet the girls at the hospital, she convinces them to stay at her house. There she offers the girls home-cooked meals, baths, conversation, and compassion.

Dion learns that Miz Lily's husband has died of a heart attack, and thinking about their own mother's death, she tells Lena that death seems to affect all people. Dion's awareness of people's humanity, regardless of race and ethnicity, is growing. Miz Lily's behavior—showing concern, compassion, and kindness—is a key factor in this process. While washing in Miz Lily's bathroom, Dion announces: "I don't want to be prejudice, Lena. [...] I don't want to be like Daddy" (65). Lena uses this as an opportune teaching moment and responds: "Good. [...] We all just people here. Me, you, Miz Lily, Larry, that waitress at Berta's. You keep that in your head, you'll be all right" (66). By entrusting their lives to Miz Lily, daring to trust across ethnic boundaries, the girls eventually find a stable home with Marie.

Significantly, the title of the first novel, *I Hadn't Meant to Tell You This*, can be interpreted in several ways. First, the title refers to Marie's promise not to tell anyone about Lena's sexual abuse or about her running away from home. However, because Marie is the narrator, and the story is told in past tense, the title can also imply that Marie has told someone Lena's secrets; after having a dream about Lena, she says, "I knew I would tell" (*Hadn't Meant* 13).

Still, if the "You" is stressed, the title refers to racism and discrimination, which is an obstacle to meaningful black/white friendships. Because of her father's prejudice, which is fueled by the history of white racism and discrimination, Marie struggles to trust Lena. If Marie did not reject her father's view and choose to see Lena as an individual, she would never have shared her personal feelings about her mother's abandonment, nor would she have told her about the secret letters she writes her mother but doesn't send. Even though Lena does not agree with her father's racist views, she is a representative white character in this text. Therefore, as a white person, she typically would not be expected to share her personal problems and feelings with a black girl. "Marie and Lena [have] move[d] with few charters into an unmapped territory of alliances between Black/White, rich/poor, into a friendship that acknowledges their differences, shares common grief, and promises a strengthened sense of self. Each girl shares what she has and borrows from the other. To achieve this, both Marie and Lena must look beyond how they are otherwise categorized and see each other as individuals" (Connolly 211). Therefore, Woodson's complex study of child abuse is enlightening because she tells the story within the context of an interracial female friendship.

While Virginia Hamilton's *A White Romance* also portrays interracial friendships and interracial relationships as complex and problematic, her depictions of interracial friendships and a relationship seem to suggest to young readers that a much more guarded approach is needed than in Woodson's works. Talley Barbour, the protagonist, is an African American teen who is being raised by her father in a predominately black urban environment, "The Neighborhood." She describes herself as a kid who "always did hang loose by herself. Everybody knew her. She talked to everyone, but she had no tight friendships" (*Romance* 29). In fact, her father, Poppy, discourages her from developing close friendships with neighborhood girls or boys, who he thinks are "fast"/promiscuous, because "... *clicks, Talley, they trouble*"—(29) and "*They ain't into nothing but gossip. They sure not into studying books. What good they going to do you, young lady? Don't even think about having some cat off the street over*" (83). Like Marie, she is growing up into a young adult without the presence of her mother. However, whereas Marie and her father communicate with each other, Talley and her father seem to maintain a more distant relationship.

Talley loves her father, a night watchman for three plants (14), who "carried a cop radio and a cop gun. Poppy made Talley [feel] safe; she loved him for it" (14–15). He gives well-intentioned directives such as the one above, which Talley at first takes to heart, but as she becomes more involved with interracial friendships and an interracial relationship, she soon ignores her father's advice. Throughout the novel, Talley rarely discusses her feelings, thoughts, or beliefs with her father; while, yes, love and respect are present, their "conversations" are generally one way—father to daughter. She says, "Parents were a screech-and-halt. Wrecks, almost, always worn-out exhausted or on the verge of flare-outs. Talley's dad could be like that" (11–12). Instead, in *A White Romance*, her peers, especially her best friend, Didi Adair, are her frame of reference and her sounding boards. The lack of in-depth communication with her father, an absent mother, and few well-developed friendships with African American peers make Talley susceptible to the negative influence of her white peers, who lead questionable lifestyles and dominant society that extols the white aesthetic of beauty and romantic love.

In *The Bluest Eye* (1970), Toni Morrison clearly illustrates the dangers for western media images for African American girls and women. Morrison clearly establishes that Pauline is an ineffective mother to Pecola because she has bought into the mass media's message that "white is right." As a young wife, Pauline frequents movie houses and futilely tries to emulate the looks of the white screen heroines. Morrison writes, "There in the dark her memory was refreshed, and she succumbed to her earlier dreams. Along with the idea of romantic love, she was introduced to another—physical beauty. Probably the most destructive ideas in the history of human thought" (122). Pauline finds escape from her own harsh social and economic realities in the fantasy world of film. She says, "'*The onliest time I be happy seem like was when I was in the picture show*'" (123). As a result, Pauline passes down a hatred of herself, her blackness, to her daughter, Pecola, who believes she will only be loved and will only find love if she possesses blue eyes, a typically Caucasian physical trait. According to bell hooks in *Black Looks*, Pauline's and Pecola's experiences and desires are not exceptional but commonplace for many African American women and girls:

> Every black woman I spoke with who was/is an ardent movie goer, a lover of the Hollywood film, testified that to experience fully the pleasure of that cinema they had to close down critique, analysis; they had to forget Racism. [...] To experience pleasure, Miss Pauline sitting in the dark must imagine herself transformed, turned into the white woman portrayed on the screen. (120–121)

Pecola and her mother Pauline learn through society to idolize the western aesthetics of romantic love and beauty and thus attempt to embrace it by any means necessary. They have nothing in their personal or cultural experiences to contradict their belief that they were unlovable and unattractive because of their dark skin. "They had looked about themselves and saw nothing to contradict the statement [that they were ugly]; saw, in fact, support for it leaning at them from every billboard, every movie, every glance" (39). Talley shares many of Pecola and Pauline's beliefs as demonstrated by her thoughts and behavior.

Talley's life changes when school officials begin to bus white students to her predominately black school, which is now a magnet school. She has not had a great deal of interaction with white teens, so when they start appearing in her school she describes them as unusual and foreign. "All those be-white kids for the first time. [...] Sounds silly now, but then, it was *strange*. White kids with pink, pimply faces and white hands and white necks, all over the place. They *smelled* different. Couldn't tell not one hand from another, nor not one face. And *blonds*. Real blond girls who looked blue they were so white" (*Romance* 29). While Talley's descriptions indicate a lack of intimate contact with white children, they do not reveal any ill will towards them because of "racial" differences. Actually, the opposite soon becomes apparent.

Talley and Didi are drawn together once they learn that they share a love of running and begin working out together. They also share the loss/absence of a parent like Marie and Lena— in this case Tally's mother, Didi's father. "Didi didn't worry about parents. She only had one now, just like Talley" (11). Interestingly, also like Marie in *I Hadn't Meant to Tell You This*, Talley becomes more aware of socio-economic status and ethnicity through her relationship with a white girl.

"[Didi and her mother] lived on the fringe … . Little row apartment houses, scrounged up, no trees to speak of. Long, long streets on the fringes of the city, where city streetcar lines ended. Edge of nowhere. […] So all be-white won't be-rich, either, and a lot of them aren't so bad, either. Lesson number one" (39). Even so, once Talley befriends Didi, whom she describes as "blond and beautiful" (43), it is soon revealed that Talley possesses an idealized view of "whiteness."

Talley is enchanted by the way Didi physically looks but also the way she behaves. She thinks, "Could've been a movie star, Didi looking that good. Furthermore, she looking at you up-front, like you there with her, she want you there. She just looked at you like you are close in with her; she cares to have you there. Her voice just straight at you—not sweet, not phony" (43). It is not a coincidence that Talley uses the term, "movie star," to describe Didi. Audiences often enjoy a movie because they identify or "force" themselves to identify with the movie protagonist, longing to be like or to be a friend of the protagonist. When Talley says that Didi "looks at you like you are close in with her; she cares to have you there," it is similar to how a movie audience member feels a connection with a film hero or heroine on the silver screen. Additionally, blond and blue-eyed physical characteristics are the epitome of a western romantic movie heroine. She also describes Didi's boyfriend, Roady, through a media context: "Kid was exotic-looking. Real dirty-blond handsome. Really pale, though. Looking like a comic-book hero with the flu" (60–61).

To expand my argument, Talley calls Didi and Roady's relationship, A White Romance (also the title of the novel) or AWR for short. She names the couple, AWR, after witnessing their openly public display of affection one day in the school hallway. "The leather dude [Roady] had cupped his hands over the angora, over Didi braless, closing and opening his hands. […] Then, his mouth was on hers. He was kissing her, all right. He ate Didi's mouth, it seemed like. His wide-open mouth covered half her face. Clear up under her nose. His eyes were closed. His hands moving down the angora, all down over Didi's no-hips" (64). The way Hamilton writes this passage indicates that Didi and Roady have a sexually active relationship. She also makes the nature of their relationship clear in other scenes in the novel. Talley and kids in the then-silent hall watch the two as if they are actors in a, "R-rated" (69), movie make-out scene until the two are forced to stop by the student patrol and school staff. Also, when Talley refers to AWR or when she watches Didi and Roady interact affectionately with one another at Roady's unkempt apartment, she often thinks, "AWR had to be some outta-sight magnificent-wonderful for everybody who saw it happen" (57), which exemplifies her desire for romantic love, her burgeoning sexual feelings, and her fantasized vision of love and sex. She says, "I wish just once to have—. That was her most secret thought. Other girls have them. So am I ugly? I wish just once—. She threw out the idea into the flow of wind and sweat. … *to have a boy*—It sailed into the air. … *likes me*" (21).

Talley's fantasy of what love, sex, romance, and a healthy relationship are are based on the romantic movie paradigm and personified by Didi and Roady. She does not have a mother or mother figure who could guide her through puberty or who could model a healthy relationship. Even Didi can see that her less-experienced friend is not ready for a serious, sexual relationship with anyone. Talley's naiveté is apparent in a conversation she has with Didi about sex.

> Didi: "No, it has to be different for everybody because everybody's different. […] Each guy and each girl, their personalities are a different combination."
> Talley: "But sex is sex. […] Wonderful is wonderful."
> Didi: "Un-uh […] If you think that … Talley, don't do it."
> Talley: "I wouldn't!"
> Didi: "You will, someday."
> Talley: "Nobody's going to love me." (56).

In this conversation, Didi tries to guide Talley in two ways. One she wants Talley to understand that sex is a natural part of life and that she will participate in it someday. This is a more open-minded view than Talley's father offers; he simply wants to protect her from negative peer groups and sexual activity with boys. She thinks, "Poppy. Man, I wouldn't dare do what Didi's up to, else Poppy kill me. And it's not wrong, like he think it something dirty. Didi's about the nicest person and she's not bad, she's not a sinner because she loves somebody" (42). Poppy's lack of effective guidance and Talley's unsophisticated view of life and love is causing her to confuse love as sex instead of sex as an expression of love. Two, Didi tries to encourage Talley to wait until she is more emotionally and psychologically mature before she becomes sexually active and will be less likely to confuse sex and love. However, like a parent who tells a child, "Do as I say, not as I do," Didi's behavior influences Talley's emotions and eventual actions more than any of her words.

In reality, Didi's and Roady's relationship is far from romantic or idyllic. Roady is a son of a prominent white family, who has fallen into a life of drug abuse and out of his family's graces. Didi is so hopelessly in love with him that she stays with him, takes care of him when he cannot take care of himself, despite the poor prognosis for a happy, fulfilling relationship. Theirs is a negatively co-dependent one. Unable to connect with her mother who is divorced from her father, Didi seeks love and a sense of security from a dysfunctional sexual relationship. Roady is attracted to Didi because she seems to love him unconditionally and takes care of him. Roady "knew everything and cared about nothing but Music and Didi, if he cared about her" (20).

It is through her inter-racial friendship with Didi, and by association with Roady, that Talley meets David Emory, a white drug dealer (although Talley does not realize this initially), begins an inter-racial relationship, and experiences her own version of A White Romance. Later in the novel, Talley and readers learn that Didi and David have had a relationship at one point and that Didi knows that he is an inappropriate boyfriend, especially for Talley. She tries to indirectly persuade Talley to not follow up on David's advances. She tells Talley, "David Emory would be a joke if he wasn't an absolute zero to begin with. [...] Talley ... well, you know what your dad will do if you mess with somebody, a white dude" (82). Didi is well aware of Poppy's suspicion, if not outright dislike of white people. He has not been supportive of Talley and Didi's friendship. Talley remembers, "The first time her Poppy had seen her running with Didi, he'd stopped dead in his tracks" (38). Talley is well aware of her father's attitudes as well.

When he learns that white students would begin going to Talley's school, he tells her, "If they white and bust in on your territory, you always got to beat them" (19). On one hand, he is saying that she as an African American will have to be twice as smart (in the classroom) and twice as fast (on the track field) to "beat"/ compete with white students because of racial discrimination. On the other hand, he is also using the word "beat" literally, meaning that she may have to physically protect herself from white student aggression. Nevertheless, Didi tries to invoke Talley's father's sentiments to protect Talley from David. Talley, however, decides to ignore Didi's warnings, thinking Didi is jealous of David's newfound interest in her. "To think a guy who once liked Didi was playing at *her*, talking to *her*" (83). She is lost in fantasy, wants to experience AWR, and dismisses Didi's disapproval. Moreover, Hamilton highlights how David is Talley's fantasy white movie hero by giving him the nickname, "Hollywood" (82).[8]

David pursues Talley, and she is flattered by the attention of a white suitor. When Talley is seduced by David, she says, "Haven't ever seen anybody like you before" (121) and thinks, "And it was true, he fascinated her" (121). Nina Mikkelsen argues that "[t]here is a social value for Talley in her relationship with David; he brings her the sense of belonging that she has not had before—an entry point into a new peer world" (Mikkelsen 79), a white world. David and Talley begin a sexual relationship, and Didi becomes resigned to the situation. At first David is attentive and loving towards Talley, yet he does give her an indication of his real personality—even in the beginning. Talley is just too blinded by inexperience and love to see. Before they have sex for the first time, David says, "Look, you want to be with me, or what? I'm not playing games with you. [...] Make up your mind, do you?" (123). He uses his words and actions to manipulate Talley although at this point, she is willing.

David not only plays psychological games with Talley but with everyone in his life. For instance, he kisses Didi in front of Talley as if to exert his power over both girls. As a drug user, Roady, the addict, is deeply involved with David, his supplier. David knows he can control Didi because she loves Roady and would not want him to cut off his supply. He knows he can control Talley because of her inexperience and her infatuation with him. Yet, Talley soon realizes this. Hamilton writes, "Talley realized that mostly, David liked controlling her. Being the one pulling her strings. He was usually in back of her or in front of her in the halls. He was by her locker before she got to it, making sure she came straight to it between classes" (134). Still, she does not end the relationship.

Didi and other kids at school can see what Talley cannot. Didi tells Talley about school gossip: "They say Talley's got the one dude she shouldn't. [...] Say he's too fast for her and too wrong. And lots of hostile stuff that you don't want to know about" (135). Eventually, it is David who ends the relationship; this was the case with Didi too. In a last-ditch effort to prolong the relationship, David takes Talley, Didi, and Roady to a Judas Priest concert, where she becomes ill and is exposed to underage drinking and more drug use.

After the night at the concert, David calls Talley less and less, and soon they are no longer meeting at his apartment. When they do meet, he is distant and irritable, picking fights. Ironically, as David fades from Talley's life, he seems to push Talley towards Victor, an African American boy who is genuinely interested in Talley. Again, David is acting as a manipulator. Didi says, "He manipulates people. [...] David put me and Roady together. He thinks he's going to put you and Victor together" (181).

Indeed, Hamilton does offer Victor as an alternative to David for Talley early in the novel, and he would easily be classified as a "catch." "Victor was the finest athlete in his formerly all-black school. And now, probably one of the best in the Magnet, if not the baddest. He was on the Student Council. [...] Nobody wanted to take him on. Victor had always been nice to Talley. She'd known him all her life. She respected him" (31). Victor is also a member of the new student patrol along with a new white male student; he is respected and holds a position of authority in the eyes of students and school officials alike. Yet, because Talley is attracted to her fantasy of what love, sex, and romance should look like—white, Talley initially rejects Victor's interest.

Once everyone in school knows about Talley's relationship with David, Victor bides his time. "Victor Davis didn't often come near Talley these days. Whenever he saw David, he froze in his tracks, staring. David knew. Kept his composure. But something was building" (135). Interestingly, Victor's body language parallels Talley's father's body language when he sees her running with Didi. The stopping and staring signifies their displeasure. Victor becomes determined to "bust" David, to catch him with drugs on the school property, and he clearly vocalizes this to Talley. "Security's going to get a dog and then we'll find where it [David's drug stash] is. [...] Tell the clown if you have to, but I'd like it to be a surprise. Talley, this is not any party-party. Everybody knows he deals. You hang with him, you'll get 'hanged' along with him" (139). This does not happen, but Victor's concern for Talley is clear.

There is a poignant scene towards the end of the novel when Talley, Roady, and Didi embrace each other, crying and trying to comfort one another. They are what David Emory has left behind, yet they do have each other. The inter-racial relationship does not work, but the inter-racial friendship is maintained. "A fine romance *they* were! Talley thought, her mouth twisting in a weak smile" (183). It is a painful, poignant scene; however, hope is re-established when Victor enters. He has followed Talley to Roady's apartment. He is that committed to trying to establish a relationship with her. There are awkward moments, but Victor is "let in" to their group.

Victor walks Talley back to The Neighborhood where they race. "In two seconds flat, he was passing her by in long, easy strides. 'uh-unh, can't,' he said, and gave her a loving look. 'Victor ... always wins'" (191). And, in this case, he finally "wins" Talley's affections. "Victor is the 'victor' of sorts. He wants Talley from the beginning, and finally he 'gets' her—or she accepts him because he loves and wants her" (Mikkelsen 78). Hamilton's choice to have Victor enter into the inter-racial world that Talley has created with Didi and Roady and then lead her back to The Neighborhood seems to suggest that Victor is taking Talley, not only spatially but emotionally back to the physical, emotional, and psychological location where she belongs. Additionally, she seems to have gained a new self-awareness from her experiences as is illustrated by her reaction to Victor's playful challenge. "Talley screeched with the giggles. Too dawn cool! No way was she going to pass him. But she stayed with him, clear to the bus stop, not even a pace behind him" (191). Symbolically, Talley has learned her own boundaries and will no longer allow another person—white or black—to set those boundaries for her, maybe *with* her, but not *for* her.

In her depictions of David and Victor, it is clear that Hamilton is telling young readers that Victor would have been Talley's best choice. David is a drug dealer; Victor is a good student and excellent athlete. Young readers learn that there are consequences for making poor choices, which Talley experiences. Hamilton clearly wants her readers to analyze and to learn how to make good decisions when selecting friends; however, why make David white when he could have just as easily been black? Why have Talley introduced to vices through her white friends, Didi and Roady? If Hamilton only wants young readers to analyze and to learn how to make the best decisions in selecting friendships and dating partners, why make the characters David, Didi, and Roady white?

On the surface, Hamilton seems to be making a statement that inter-racial friendships and relationships are not healthy for growing, impressionable young African American girls. However, underlining this reading, I believe is a more complex statement from Hamilton. While I do not believe Hamilton is trying to encourage her young readers to reject inter-racial friendships or relationships, I do believe that she is asking them to seriously consider *why* they chose to cross ethnic boundaries for love and friendship. Talley, for example, crosses ethnic boundaries because she believes/confuses "true" love and friendship as only qualifying when they are primarily with white peers. I believe that Hamilton may also be highlighting the possibility that inter-racial friendships may be more easily maintained than inter-racial relationships as demonstrated by the end of *A White Romance*. Although she is wounded, Talley grows through her experiences like any protagonist in a bildungsroman and is more mature by the end of this particular life journey.

Both Woodson and Hamilton portray inter-racial friendships and/or relationships with complex characters who face major life challenges. Marie and Lena establish a relationship because of the commonality of absent mothers. Talley and Didi also have a connection because of a missing parent. Marie's friendship enables Lena to overcome her father's abuse, and Didi's friendship enables Talley to withstand her feelings of worthlessness when David leaves her. They are able to offer emotional support to one another when other peers, and sometimes the remaining parent, have been unable to do so. Establishing friendships and intimate relationships is one of the most important and sometimes heart-wrenching experiences for adolescents, and those who cross ethnic borders have to face other obstacles to developing relationships as well.

In their novels, Woodson and Hamilton reveal to their young readers some of the hardships encountered by those in these relationships, Hamilton arguably in a more painful way than Woodson. Yet, simultaneously, they are encouraging their readers, despite difficulties, to also be open to inter-racial friendships and/or relationships because their novels show that ultimately all people have more in common than not. The writers only hope, especially Hamilton, that young, African American girls who do choose to be in inter-racial friendships and/or relationships do so for the right reasons.

6

Dealing with Death: Candy Dawson Boyd's *Breadsticks and Blessing Places* and *Circle of Gold*

Death is a topic that few of us actually choose to discuss although it is an inevitable part of life. The death of a loved one is a difficult life event for anyone to experience, let alone a child. However, children have experienced and are experiencing the loss of a parent, a sibling, or a friend every day and must come to terms with the grief process.[1] "From the beginning of their lives, children have the capacity to observe the world around them. They observe many things that they cannot name. Thus, they may make sense of the cycle of life and death but not yet have words for it. [...] They learn that people grow old and die, but they may not learn how to acknowledge and deal with their sadness and what this loss means to them" (Silverman 2). Oftentimes, the child will need the emotional support of the remaining parent, family friends, and/or peers.

In this chapter, I study how African American writer, Candy Dawson Boyd, depicts death in her young adult novels and helps assist her readers in understanding and dealing with this aspect of life. I focus on her two novels, *Circle of Gold* (1984) and *Breadsticks and Blessing Places* (1985), and analyze Boyd's portrayals of the unique pressures Mattie and Toni, respectively, experience in their homes and at school when a parent or close friend passes away. Boyd illustrates the girls' need for emotional support from the remaining parent and/or a substitute figure (typically a woman) and their peers to cope.

Mattie and Toni are best friends, and both appear in each of the novels. Mattie is the protagonist in *Circle of Gold*, and Toni is the protagonist in the sequel, *Breadsticks and Blessing Places*. Mattie is the first to live through the grief process when her father dies. Toni will not understand the extent of pain that Mattie has experienced until she goes through her own experience with death. "Shame swept over Toni, making her blush in the cold. They had been best friends, and Mattie had been forced to hide her true feelings. Toni knew why. She hadn't wanted to know or to hear. It had been too terrifying to believe that she could lose her father or mother" (*Breadsticks* 157). Mattie will be an important source of guidance and strength for Toni when it is her turn in the next novel.

In *Circle of Gold*, Mattie is coping with the passing of her father. "The death of a parent is one of the most fundamental losses a child can face. Ideally, parents support their children, both physically and emotionally; they provide a stable home environment in which children can grow and mature; and they serve both as the children's protectors and as their models" (Worden 9). Indeed, the stability in Mattie's home has disappeared. Her mother, Mrs. Benson, runs the apartment building where they live and also works part-time jobs to provide for the family. Mattie's twin brother, Matt, has a paper route, and Mattie baby-sits. Everyone must contribute to the family's income now. Additionally, Mattie and Matt, have taken on major household duties such as cooking meals to help their mother. Consequently, there is little family time. And, lately, Mrs. Benson is easily agitated with the children, especially Mattie. She even hits Mattie out of frustration at one point.

Mattie believes that her mother constantly finds fault with her because Matt is her mother's favorite, and she had been her father's favorite. Even though Matt says it is not true, Mattie believes their mother loves him more, believing their mother's preference is just more obvious now. At times, she remembers that her father called her "African princess, lovely African princess, carrying the leaves of the gingko tree like a dozen golden fans on top of my head" (90). His words, his photograph, and his memory comfort Mattie throughout the novel. Her father made her feel special and like a beautiful black girl. She has never doubted his love, and it continues to sustain her—even after his death. To gain her mother's love, Mattie works and saves money to buy Mrs. Benson an expensive pin for Mother's Day. She even enters a newspaper writing contest to earn money. She tells Matt, "I'm set on the pin. It's *the* special gift. I have to get it for her" (63).

Mrs. Stamps, a neighbor and elder friend who sometimes functions as a supplemental mother figure for Mattie in this novel and for Toni in the next, tries to warn Mattie that "the pin is not going to solve all [her] family's problems" (96). When Mrs. Stamps asks her what she would do if she were not able to purchase the pin, Mattie says, "I'd want to die" (97), revealing the overemphasis she has placed on the pin's meaning. Mrs. Stamps uses the situation as a teaching moment: "Mattie, you may be letting yourself in for a big disappointment. On the other hand, this may wind up being the triumph of your young life. You have to accept the risks" (97). Mattie wants to win so badly that she even asks Toni, a better writer, to write an essay for her; Toni reluctantly agrees because they are friends and because she knows how important winning is to Mattie. Mattie has to decide whether or not to send in Toni's or her own essay to the contest. It is an ethical dilemma and an opportunity for Boyd to teach young readers to choose to do right even if the choice has to be made under difficult circumstances.

After mailing in the essay, Mattie discusses her predicament with Mrs. Stamps who does not want to know which essay was mailed but says that she trusts that Mattie made the right decision. "Mattie, whatever you decided is done. You have to live with the consequences. If you made the right decision, though, you may be in for some good, skin-stretching times" (102). In other words, Mrs. Stamps lets her know that by making the right decision on her own, she would be demonstrating that she is maturing into a responsible young adult. In fact, Mattie does make the right decision; she sends in her own essay. Her words express her entire experience—with her mother and father—well and illustrate that despite adversity she is growing up and becoming a stronger individual.

> Dear Mr. Phillips,
>
> My name is Mattie Mae Benson. My father is dead. My mother loves my twin brother, Matt, more than me. I love my mother but I have a hard time telling her. I wanted to win this contest so much that I asked my best friend, Toni, to write an essay. I thought I had a better chance to win with her essay. I'm so bad with words. If I could only sing and tell you how I feel about my mother, I could win. I want to win the money so I can buy my mother a beautiful pearl and gold pin at Stern's. It is beautiful and special, just like my mother. This is the essay. I'm sending it to you because I love my mother in good times and bad times. But I love her too much to try to win with a lie.
>
> Sincerely and truthfully,
> Mattie Mae Benson (131).

By the end of the novel, the reader learns that Mattie ties for first place with another child, and instead of giving her prize money, the newspaper officials buy the pin for her and present it to Mrs. Benson. Mrs. Benson quickly lets her daughter know how much she loves her, but she also sees how her behavior has negatively affected Mattie. She tells her mother, "I just wanted you to know how sad I feel when you cry and miss Daddy and call for Matt and not me" (131). Mrs. Benson reassures her, "You are mine—my only girl" (132). Mrs. Benson is able to embrace Mattie and offer reassurance because she has finally begun her own healing process.

Even so, Mattie must first undertake a major emotional journey and goes to such lengths because she can sense that she has figuratively "lost" her mother because her mother's depression over her husband's death renders her an ineffective parent. Mrs. Benson cannot help her children cope with their grief because she has not dealt with her own. Consequently, Mattie and Matt often do not want to burden their mother with their fears and anxiety; instead, they try to protect and care for their mother. The children take on the parental role, worrying about their mother's mental state, eating routine, and habitual headaches. Mattie turns to Mrs. Stamps for comfort and counsel after her mother hits her. Mrs. Stamp explains the difficulties—financial and otherwise—her mother is facing: "Your mother is under a lot of pressure. She's not herself, child" (55). She tells Mattie, "I think your mother needs to talk to someone, to help her through this hard time. The pastor, or a counselor." [...] These are the times to hold on to your faith. This is when loving your mother really counts" (55). Acting on Mrs. Stamps' advice, Mattie urges Matt to ask their minister, Reverend Harris, to speak to their mother. However, their mother becomes angry and blames Mattie for telling her business. She says, "What do you mean talking to Reverend Harris about me? I know Matt did the talking, but you put him up to it, didn't you, Mattie?" (64) and "You went outside this family and told our business, Mattie. I should whip you for that" (64). Matt stops his mother, yelling, "Mama, stop it. You're ready to hit Mattie again, when all she tried to do was help you. We didn't know what to do" (64). Their mother realizes soon after this incident that she needs help coping, and she acknowledges this to Mattie. "'Mattie, I'm sorry for hitting you and screaming at you. Reverend Harris is right. You and Matt are right. So is your friend Mrs. Stamps. I do need to talk to somebody,' She sighed and rubbed her forehead. 'I'm so tired, always so tired and worried'" (73). Mrs. Benson seeks professional help from a therapist although she does not reveal this to the children immediately. Silverman suggests that "[i]ndividual counseling ... provid[es] a safe space to talk and have feelings legitimated" (205). Mrs. Benson would greatly benefit from discussing her emotional state with a professional.

After some months of counseling, Mrs. Benson tells Mattie that the therapist, "Mrs. Potter is a good woman and she's helping me deal with your Daddy's death—and being responsible for raising you two alone" (121). Mrs. Benson begins going on special shopping trips with Mattie and taking Mattie and Matt on outings such as going to the movies. "It was like old times standing in the popcorn line in the movie theater and fussing about how close to sit. [...] Mattie couldn't quite believe all the fun they were having. Matt winked at her. Mama was actually laughing" (106). Mrs. Benson has to reestablish stability in her home, return a sense of normalcy to her children's lives, and take back the role of parent; she is not able to do so until she confronts her own despair and begins her own healing process. "To help children in [the grief] process, we must confront our own fears and begin to search for the words we do not have. We cannot teach children what we do not know" (Silverman 4). Because she could not cope with her husband's death, she certainly is not in a position to guide her children through the experience. Mrs. Benson must be the responsible adult so that Mattie and Matt will have the opportunity to be children. Yes, their lives have changed because of their father's death, but if their mother can help them negotiate through this time, they have a better chance of recovery. As a result, young readers learn their parents, like Mrs. Benson, are human beings, who feel pain and make mistakes. They also learn the importance of asking for help to cope after the loss of a loved one.

An important example of Mrs. Benson reestablishing herself in the parental role is her defense of Mattie at school. In a subplot, two girls, Angel and Charlene, bully Mattie at school because she is smart and will not let Angel copy her work. When Angel's bracelet is stolen, she accuses Mattie. Their teacher and most of the students believe that she is guilty, so she and Toni devise a plan to prove her innocence. Toni pretends she is no longer friends with Mattie and befriends Angel and Charlene until they discover the true identity of the thief. Eventually, the reader learns that Charlene has taken Angel's bracelet, and Mattie is vindicated. However, what is more important to Mattie is that her mother believes in her innocence from the beginning and stands up for her during a meeting with her teacher and Angel's parents. Angel and Mattie are present during this meeting, and "[a]fter the meeting Mattie hug[s] her mother" (108). To Mattie, her mother's support and belief in her shows that her mother loves and cares for her. In this case, Mrs. Benson is acting as a parent and protector.

The title of the novel, *Circle of Gold*, is significant here because it represents family to Mattie. Gold is a priceless metal, and family is a priceless entity. When Mattie's father dies, the family's circle of gold is broken. While Mrs. Benson is unable to perform parental duties, the circle remains broken. However, once Mrs. Benson seeks and accepts help, she is able to mend the family. The family is not and never will be the same, but Mrs. Benson is able to reform a new one, a new circle of gold for Matt and Mattie. At the end of the novel, Mattie can sense that their family has completed a painful phase of life and endured.

Whereas Boyd shows young readers how a parent/child relationship is reshaped by the death of a parent in *Circle of Gold*, in *Breadsticks and Blessing Places*, she illustrates how a child handles losing a close friend. Toni exhibits great emotional distress after the death of one of her two best friends, Susan, who is killed by a drunk driver. When her parents tell her that Susan has died, Toni goes into denial. "No, she's not dead. I want to see Susan! Daddy, stop this" (*Breadsticks* 86). At one point in the novel, she even prays to God to "please bring Susan back" (96). Her parents decide to keep her out of school for a few days because of her distress.

One of the main reasons that Toni is so upset is because Susan, in some ways, has become a closer friend to her than even Mattie. When Toni begins menstruation, she shares this information with Susan not Mattie because Mattie has not begun her period. Although Toni's mother has already prepared her for this moment—"[o]n a hot Sunday last August, when just she an her mother were home, they had talked about her growing up, starting her menstrual cycle, and learning how to change her napkins, and keep herself clean" (43), Toni wants to also share this event with an experienced peer. Her anxiety and excitement are obvious in the conversation she has with Susan during a holiday party.

Toni: I got *it.*
Susan: It? What's it? Come on, we'll miss the party.
Toni: What you got last spring.
Susan: You mean you got your period? [...] Are you sure?
Toni: Don' be dumb! I'm sure.
Susan: That's amazing. How do you feel?
Toni: Different. I don't like this, Susan. My stomach hurts, down here. [...] And the sanitary napkin feels real strange. Can you see anything? I mean, can you tell? I'd die if anybody could tell!
Susan: Nope.
Toni: I don't like walking.
Susan: Don't worry. I've had seven so far. Did you bring some extras? Mine wasn't much the first two times. You want aspirin? [...] Mother Dear (her grandmother) (sic) gives me tea with honey and puts the heating pad on my stomach. You know, here.
Toni: I brought two napkins with me, see? [...] How do you keep from-I mean, how do you know when to change, so nothing happens?
Susan: Well, at first I looked all the time, every hour. But it depends on how fast you flow. Just check yourself. [...] Now we're both grown. (*Breadsticks* 48).

As the conversation illustrates, Susan reassures Toni about her menstruation experience and answers questions she may be too embarrassed to ask an adult. Toni freely expresses herself with Susan, and they have bonded, moving into maturation together. This is a powerful time in a girl's life and one that she only wants to share with her closest confidants. Susan fits this description for Toni, and her loss is felt by Toni deeply.

When she does return to school, she notices that "[e]very sign that Susan Lawrence had been a student in Room 308 was gone" (90). Susan's desk is empty, and her name has been removed from the coat rack. Toni yells at her teacher, Mrs. Swallow, "'Where are Susan's things?' demanded Toni, not addressing her teacher by name. 'Why isn't her name on the coat hook? Who took her things?'" (90). Mrs. Swallow realizes that Toni is not handling Susan's death well and is acting-out as a means of coping. "Acting-out behavior in bereaved children may be a part of normal grieving" (Worden 152). Toni's acting-out seems to escalate, lashing out verbally at classmates, even Mattie.[2]

Soon, Toni is no longer disrespectful to her teacher, but her anger and pain are also displayed in other ways. "When we think of bereaved people, we think of tears, immense sadness, a sense of heaviness in the body, despair, and great stress. In fact, feelings after a death are dynamic and changing all the time" (Silverman 23).[3] Toni's ability to concentrate on school work is negatively affected, and she cannot focus on preparing for the King Academy test. King Academy is a magnet school that her parents want her to attend. Her father even takes her to the University of Chicago's campus to motivate her. He explains to her that he and her mother want her to study and earn a good education because she is an African American in the United States. "You have to get a good education to make it in this troubled society, and sometimes even that isn't enough. [...] Now, what you do with that education is your business, but your mother and I want you to have the tools to make a good future for yourself" (*Breadsticks* 73). Initially, Toni is not interested in going to King, but after a trip to the academy and meeting some of the students, she decides she does want to go. When she decides that she wants to attend King, not because her parents want her to but because she wants to, she finds the inspiration to pull herself out of her grief over Susan's death. For instance, when she takes the King entrance exam, she uses the meditation technique one of the King students has taught her to manage test anxiety. So, when thoughts of Susan begin to cloud her mind, Toni tells herself, "No, I can't think about her now. I have to think about scoring high enough to get into King" (199). She has taken Mrs. Stamps advice—to keep living.

Like Mattie, Toni turns to Mrs. Stamps for comfort, understanding, and wisdom. Mrs. Stamps shares with Toni her own personal experience with death; this lets Toni know that she can believe what Mrs. Stamps says about death because she has gone through it. She has lost every member of her immediate family. Toni is shocked and asks how she can endure the loss of so many family members. Mrs. Stamps says, "I took the time to mourn in my own way. [...] And I decided to let that person go and keep the memories in my heart. I made myself return to the business of living" (167). Mrs. Stamps believes that it is the responsibility of those left behind to *actively* decide to move forward with their own lives. "You have to make your own peace, and that takes doing, not sitting around and moping. *Doing*" (168). The stress on the word, "doing," highlights that moving out of grief is an active, conscious decision/choice. When Toni seeks peer counsel in this case, she turns to Mattie, remembering that Mattie has recently lost her father, and finds that her suggestion supports Mrs. Stamps' suggestion.[4]

At first, Mattie is reluctant to share her coping method and makes Toni promise not to tell anyone else. She says, "Just because my father died doesn't qualify me as an expert" (150). However, since she is trying to be there for Toni during her time of grief, Mattie cannot avoid reopening her own grief over her father's death.[5] Even so, Mattie assists Toni. Both girls are learning the hard lesson that it is not always easy to be a friend. Toni has learned this when she helped Mattie clear her name about the bracelet and reluctantly wrote the essay for Mattie. Mattie is now learning the depths of friendship because she is supporting Toni in spite of her own wounds.

After Toni attends and participates with her classmates in Susan's funeral, she still does not feel closure. Mattie says that she felt the same way after her father died, so she held her own secret ceremony. "'After the funeral, I kept up my schoolwork and all, but inside I was a mess. So I had my own special funeral for my daddy. Just me [...],' Mattie stressed. 'I planned the service.'" (169). By creating her own service for her father, Mattie actively engaged/confronted her father's death. Since his real grave "is far away and I can't get there on the bus. I took some things and made him special presents. I went to a place in the park that we used to go to, under a ginkgo tree." (170). During the service, Mattie buries the presents and sings his favorite songs. "[W]henever I really need to, I go there and sit awhile [...] When I leave, I feel better" (170).[6] From Mattie's example, young readers learn that a loved one does not have to be forgotten in order to ease their sorrow. After their discussion, Mattie pushes Toni to "unstick" (170) herself but leaves Toni to decide on how she will do so. Like Mrs. Stamps, Mattie stresses that it is up to the individual to actively choose to begin living again.

Participating in ritual—viewing the body, attending a funeral—is an important step for a person to move toward the acceptance that a loved one has passed. Toni's parents insist that she attend Susan's; however, like Mattie she feels that those services are more for the adults. She decides to create her own good-bye ceremony, her own "blessing place" for Susan. However, her service, unlike Mattie's (Mattie is more private and does not make friends as easily as Toni.),[7] includes Mrs. Stamps, Carl—Toni's younger brother—and Mattie, the people she has been the most open and honest about her feelings with throughout this ordeal. During the service in Mrs. Stamps' dining room, she asks that everyone write something nice about Susan and then read it out loud. Afterwards, she burns their messages in a pot as an acknowledgment of Susan's existence and death; the ashes represent Susan's actual ashes—"ashes to ashes and dust to dust," words often said at a funeral ceremony. Next, Toni asks Mattie to sing a song, an action that finally connects the two. She has always wanted Mattie and Susan to be close friends, but that kind of relationship never materialized. By asking Mattie to sing a song, her way of expressing herself, specifically for Susan, Toni gives Mattie a chance to sing words of friendship that she never was able to say to Susan while she was alive and to say a heart-felt good-bye. The little group eats birthday cake because the ceremony is held on Susan's birthday. In doing so, they celebrate her birth and her life as well as grieve her death.

Next, Mrs. Stamps drives her to the lake where Toni scatters the ashes of their messages in the direction of Jackson, Mississippi—Susan's burial site. Finally, she places items that remind her of Susan such as one of the Statue of Liberty earrings Susan has given her and breadsticks in remembrance of how happy Susan said she had been eating breadsticks with her father[8] in her own music box and throws it into the lake. "When the tinkling music was loudest and clearest, she cast the box out, watching it bob on the waves until she could not longer see it" (193). Toni has finally said good-bye to her grief. Subsequently, Toni tells Mrs. Stamps, "I still feel sad. But I don't feel so stuck. I did something for Susan my way. [...] Nobody can make me forget her. She was my best friend" (193). Toni has closure. She now can hold onto her memories of Susan without letting them interrupt her life.

Boyd's vivid, fictional depictions of grief and how it can affect the lives of young African American girls are poignant. *Circle of Gold* and *Breadsticks and Blessing Places* delve into a subject many adults do not like to think about, and even fewer want to discuss with their children, and stress the importance of the presence of peers, extended family, and non-family members in the lives of grieving young people. Adults can use these novels as teaching tools that provide a platform for honest discussions about death and how to manage its aftereffects.

7

The Bling-Bling Generation: Celebrity, Commercialism, and Consumerism in Deborah Gregory's *The Cheetah Girls: Livin' Large*

In the last two decades, hip-hop culture and rap music have become dominant forces in the American music industry and popular culture, and with massive global promotion from the music industry, this once-marginalized music form has become an international phenomenon.[1] The voices and images of young, urban, African American men and women, once a silenced and invisible minority, are now transmitted through radios and Ipods, along with their music videos across millions of television screens around the world. Hip hop has become a global commodity indeed. However, because these young people have gained a national and international stage/platform for their thoughts and concerns, one must ask some serious questions of the culture and the people who produce and sell it to the young masses. For instance, what do hip-hop artists have to say about social, political, and economic issues concerning people of color in the United States and the world? How do the images hip-hop artists create through their music videos influence the way the dominant culture and the world perceive African Americans?

And, finally, how do hip-hop artists' lyrics and video images influence the perceptions, values, and self-images of young people?

Studying the effects of mass media on children and young adults is not new. Since the mid-twentieth century, social critics, psychologists, and sociologists, among others, have been studying the influential role of mass media, especially television, film, and popular music, on developing minds.[2] Increasingly, more academics are examining the influence of the hip-hop lifestyle as depicted in music lyrics and music videos, on youth.[3] In this chapter, I analyze Deborah Gregory's hip-hop-infused, young adult book series, *The Cheetah Girls* and the effects of hip-hop culture as represented in lifestyle, music lyrics, and music video images on the minds of young African American girls. I also will primarily focus on aspects of the first four books of the series, *Wishing on a Star* (1999), *Shop in the Name of Love* (1999), *Who's 'Bout to Bounce?* (1999), and *Hey, Ho, Hollywood!* (1999), which are now in a compiled edition called *The Cheetah Girls: Livin' Large* (2003). I have chosen to limit myself to the first four books because they are the foundation of the series and set the initial hip-hop language, style, and character of the series.

First, I will briefly discuss the evolution of rap music and hip-hop culture to establish a historical context for my discussion of the novels. Scholars and music journalists such as Nelson George and Tricia Rose have documented and analyzed the rise of rap music and hip-hop culture in essays and book-length works.[4] In the mid-1970s, many young, urban, African Americans began to realize that promises of economic, social, and political power that were supposed to have been derived from the gains of the American civil rights movement had passed them by. Instead, they were trapped in inner-city ghettos with rising poverty rates and inferior public schools. Simultaneously, many upwardly mobile blacks and their white counterparts left the urban centers and resettled in surrounding suburbs. By the 1980s, many American urban centers looked like segments of some Third-World countries. Increasingly high crime rates, teen pregnancies, school drop-out rates, and drug use plagued inner-city residents. Yet, in the "Just Say No," "Don't Worry Be Happy," Reagan 1980s few cared, listened to, or addressed the concerns of this marginalized group.

Young people have always found a discourse to express their needs and frustrations about the world around them, especially in the African American community. The hip-hop generation is not an exception. Young African Americans found their voices through a new form of music and established their own lyrical heroes and spokesmen, rappers. Grandmaster Flash, Mellie Mel, Rakim, and Big Daddy Kane are a few of the lyrical heroes who became voices for the marginalized and for a generation of hip hoppers. These "old school" rappers were like blues singers of the more distant past who expressed the pain and frustrations of an oppressed people through their music.[5] Rap had become a contemporary version of the blues voice in the African American musical and literary/vernacular tradition.[6] Many of the "old school" rappers had messages from and for "the people," the African American working and underclass, to share to the world in hopes of improving the lives of inner-city residents.

As the music gained in popularity and the music video media outlets such as Music Television (MTV) began to play videos by black artists[7] and Black Entertainment Television Network (BET) joined the cable television lineup, more American youth began to listen to these artists and to emulate their images. In the mid-1980s, Run DMC, a rap group collaborated with the 1970s rock group, Aerosmith, on a remake of Aerosmith's hit song, "Walk This Way" and corresponding video. Their rap-rock alliance not only brought about Aerosmith's comeback to the music industry but also bridged the worlds of rap and rock and brought rap into the American mainstream in a major way.

In the late 1980s and early 1990s, gangsta rappers like Niggas with Attitudes (NWA) and Ice T unabashedly told tales of surviving the street life in ghettos, police brutality, and gang violence. Although profanity had been used in some previous rap lyrics, these groups increased the use of profanity, graphic depictions of street violence, graphic depictions of sex, and negative epitaphs for black women such as "bitches" and "hoes." As a result, congresspersons and people such as C. Delores Tucker spoke against this music and sought to censor it. "In 1993, her friends [R&B artists] Dionne Warwick and Melba Moore gave Tucker an opportunity to climb … into the spotlight when they approached her about having [her lobbying group] the [National Political Congress of Black Women] NPCBW take up the fight against gangsta rap" (Chang 452).[8]

However, as rap music and the images became increasingly mainstream and a money-generating marvel, the music industry began mass-producing artists, some with questionable rapping skills, who could produce and sell rap songs that talked about the "good life," portraying themselves as money- and women-drawing magnets.[9] In their videos, they portrayed a lifestyle of easy women, harmless marijuana use, flowing champagne, flashy designer clothing, and sparkling diamonds. The portrayal of women increasingly became demeaning, objectifying women as sexual objects often focusing on certain body parts like the "booty" and the breasts. These artists "ditched the inner-city blues for more smoothed-out roughness and gangsta parties, and sold even more records. […] The disposable could become the indispensable. The Black thing you once couldn't understand had now become the G thang you could buy into" (Chang 420–421). Hip Hop becomes an international phenomenon and a major force in the music industry, producing major money for the industry.

Gregory's novels demonstrate positive and negative aspects of hip-hop culture. One of the positive aspects exhibited in the novels is ethnic diversity. For example, although rap music and hip-hop culture were originally derived from the creative minds of urban African Americans, the music and culture have been embraced by youth of various ethnicities and nationalities. In *Can't Stop Won't Stop: A History of the Hip-Hop Generation*, Jeff Chang states, "To me, hip-hop says, 'Come as you are.' We are a family. [...] I think hip-hop has bridged the cultural gap. It brings white kids together with Black kids, brown kids with yellow kids. They have something in common that they love. It gets past (sic) the stereotypes and people hating each other because of those stereotypes" (xi). In *Why White Kids Love Hip-Hop: Wankstas, Wiggers, Wannabes, and the New Reality of Race in America*, Bakari Kitwana more directly postulates that hip hop has changed the racial landscape of America: "today's acceptance of hip-hop as mainstream popular culture has radically altered the racial landscape. And in that nebulous space where hip-hop and popular culture meet, we see specific shifts in the ways young Americans are processing race" (xii).

By highlighting this aspect of hip-hop culture, Gregory embraces a postmodern sense of ethnicity. Three of the five young protagonists in *The Cheetah Girls* series are bi- or multiracial. The founder and leader of The Cheetah Girls, Galleria Garibaldi, is of African American and Italian heritage. Chanel Coco Cristalle Duarte Rodriquez Domingo Simmons is described as "a blend of Dominican and Puerto Rican on her mother's side, Jamaican and Cuban on her father's side" (*Wishing on a Star* 7). Later in the book series, readers learn that Dorinda Rogers, a foster child who does not know her parents, is of African American and Caucasian descent. Gregory is acknowledging America's "changing racial landscape" in her novels. She knows that bi- and multiracial identity is a part of the lived reality of many children and young adults who are products of or have friends who are products of inter-racial relationships.

Moreover, Galleria and Chanel are proud of their mixed heritage and do not seem to suffer from any ethnic identity conflicts; instead, they accept them all. For example, Galleria's urban argot signifies her identification with her African American heritage while her use of Italian such as informing the readers that "un bacio" is Italian for a kiss reveals her affection for her father and her identification with her Italian heritage. "In some ways, her characters are cutting edge. They imply an emerging trend in children's and young adult literature, the biracial and multiracial character who signifies a possible new societal order"

(Harris 227). By doing so, she is teaching her young readers to be more excepting of themselves and their various ethnic backgrounds and teaching others racial tolerance.[10]

Additionally, it must be noted that each of the books is narrated by a different member of the Cheetah Girls—Galleria in *Wishing on a Star*, Chanel in *Shop in the Name of Love*, Dorinda in *Who's 'Bout to Bounce?*, and Aquanette—speaking only for herself yet representing her twin's (Aginette's) perspective too—in *Hey, Ho, Hollywood!*. By essentially giving each member her own narrative, so that each can offer her own perspective on the group and each other, Gregory stresses to her readers that while a group can form a powerful unit, the members do not have to give up their individuality. With this literary technique, Gregory seems to be further commenting on ethnic identity; her bi- and multi-racial characters embrace all of their ethnic heritage and do not simply choose one ethnic group or the other. Thus, the message for young readers seems to be that diversity and individuality can coexist within a group, musical or ethnic.

Another positive aspect of hip-hop culture that is unique to *The Cheetah Girl* series is their creative use of urban dialect. In fact, the girls have their own Cheetah language that is derivative of urban language but unique to them. The Cheetah Girls Glossary at the end of each book reinforces the argot as a legitimate youth language for the readers and makes the Cheetah Girls seem more real. Readers can use the language themselves to more closely identify with the characters. For example, at the end of *Who's About to Bounce?* the glossary contains "At the end of her rope-a-dope—To run out of moves. When you wanna give up," "Bounce—To leave. To jet. To go away and come back another day," and "Diggable Planet—A cool place" (409). A unique, common language increases the bond between the girls in The Cheetah Girls group and the bond between the readers and the characters. Readers can also use the special vocabulary to connect with other Cheetah fans and to identity with the Cheetah "world"/ "lifestyle."

Another positive aspect of the Cheetah series is the attitude about body image. Although Galleria is not the thinnest of the girls, she is not obsessed with her weight.[11] This is significant for young female readers who are bombarded by airbrushed photographs of thin, perfectly symmetrical, and white or "light" celebrities and models in magazines, on television, and in film. Additionally, Galleria's mother, Dorothea, is a "size-eighteen, class-A diva" (*Wishing* 10), who sales high fashion in plus sizes in her fashion boutique, "Toto in New York … Fun in Diva Sizes"(*Wishing* 7). Dorothea is comfortable with her weight and body image. As a result, she passes on the same mentality to Galleria.

Even so, Gregory's characters also possess negative aspects of contemporary hip-hop culture; "[d]espite hip-hop's pervasive presence in American life, it is still the scapegoat for declining American values" (Kitwana 19) as exemplified by some aspects of *The Cheetah Girls* series. For example, The Cheetah Girls have adopted and/or desire the "bling-bling" lifestyle, one based on commercialism, consumerism, and materialism, which is often glorified through rap/hip-hop soul music lyrics and videos. Although Chang believes that "[hip hop] ain't about bling bling" (xi), many contemporary artists believe it is and that hip hop is not only a means to express their innermost feelings but also a means to escape poverty and to acquire and display material wealth. Public intellectual Kevin Powell explains it this way: "hip-hop culture is often confused with the hip-hop industry, and the consequences have been catastrophic for my generation and the generation directly behind me" (61). In *Check It While I Wreck It: Black Womanhood, Hip-Hop Culture, and the Public Sphere*, Gwendolyn D. Pough posits that ownership of material things such as designer clothes, cars, and jewelry is a mark of "authenticity" to the Hip-Hop Generation, generally those born after the American civil rights movement began.

> This authenticity check serves a dual function. It is a check to see if the gear [designer clothing] and jewelry the person is wearing are real and not knock-off clothing or fake jewelry. And it is also a check on the person to see if he or she really belongs. The authenticity check becomes a self-monitoring that pushes members of the Hip-Hop generation to acquire as many things as they can in order to fully belong. [...] [M]embers of the Hip-Hop generation [rely] on physical appearance and material things for image, without which they feel less than worthy. (147)

Rap artists often wear ostentatious pieces of diamond jewelry, "ice," list expensive designer labels such as Versace and pricey cars such as Bentleys in their music lyrics, and throw money in the air in music videos. All markers demonstrate to the world that they are now successful individuals who have obtained the American Dream, sometimes, it is implied, by dubious means. From an economic standpoint, hip hop has become an agent for the capitalist market by helping to create a generation of consumers. "At the same time, mass marketers were scrambling to re-establish brand preeminence. Advertising budgets were plunging, as aging white baby boomers opted for value over brand. [...][A]s companies like Nike, Adidas, and Pepsi searched for new markets, they discovered that urban youth of color—until then an ignored niche—were a more brand-conscious, indeed brand-leading, demographic than they had ever realized" (Chang 417). Forget the white house with a picket fence and a Cadillac in the garage; now, it's a mansion with several Rolls-Royces in the ten-car garage.

Americans are infamous for the desire to "keep up with the Jones," but for impressionable children and young adults who are seeking acceptance and a psychological space to belong, who are bombarded by the ghetto-fabulous images, and who are encouraged by peers to "fit" into their generation, this situation can lead to a lifestyle of debt. I do not believe that it is a coincidence that in the last 10 years young adults have become "Young, Fabulous, and Broke."[12] Nonexistent savings accounts, maxed-out credit cards, ballooning mortgages, student loans, and expensive car leases, all allow young adults to look successful well before they actually are.

Granted, hip hop is not the sole reason that consumerism, a culture of immediate gratification, has taken over the American mindset. However, hip-hop culture has been co-opted and has become a marketing dream, selling everything from clothing to perfume, telling young African Americans how to be successful and how to obtain the American Dream. Hip-hop artists' conspicuous consumption of "trophy" items teaches young adults by example that a successful person must possess great wealth and flaunt it. However, the reality is that the average teen will not gain fame or great wealth, yet they may feel unsuccessful in life if their lifestyle does not match their heroes. Some may turn to illegal means in order to live a moneyed existence. Powell argues that in today's popular culture "there is virtually nothing countering these destructive lyrics and images" (61), and Gregory's book series actually reinforces the materialistic aspirations of many persons in hip-hop culture and influences young readers because her books are "strongly linked to popular culture and consumerism" (Harris 218).

For example, Galleria, in particular, wears the latest designer clothes and accessories such as "Gucci loafers" (*Wishing* 53). Chanel uses her mother's credit card to purchase a performance outfit for Dorinda and to make excessive purchases for herself without her mother's permission in *Shop in the Name of Love*. In actuality, Chanel is acting passive-aggressively to express her anger at her mother's lack of support for her dreams of singing fame and at her mother's negative attitude towards her father whom she has divorced and his new wife. Still, the fact that her mother has a credit card and her father has established several salons for his new wife indicates a certain level of economic power. Anginette and Aquanette's divorced parents are managerial executives with Avon. The girls can afford to maintain up-to-date hairstyles and stylized, manicured nails. Galleria, Chanel, Anginette, and Aquanette are also members of the Kats and Kittys Klub, based on the real Jack and Jill organization, which is a social club/organization for children of affluent African Americans.

For the most part, The Cheetah World is one of economic privilege, and to a certain extent, one of glamour. By creating this type of Cheetah World, Gregory celebrates and, more importantly, validates these values and lifestyle choices in the eyes of young readers. This can have major consequences for young African American girls. One of her characters, Dorinda, is a possible example. She notices the socio-economic differences between herself and her friends. She is a foster child and has a part-time job with the YMCA even though she is a year under the legal working age. For a time, she never lets the girls visit her home in the Cornwall Projects because she says, "after seeing where *they* all live, I'm embarrassed to let them see my home" (*Bounce* 272–273). Young readers who do not have the socio-economic means to live the Cheetah Girl lifestyle may feel inferior to peers who can, and still others may try unscrupulous means to gain the lifestyle. While Gregory seems to address this issue somewhat with Dorinda's struggle to truly feel comfortable and a part of the other girls' social and economic world, the overall sense of the books is that an affluent and glamorous lifestyle is the best and the one to seek. After all, if and when The Cheetah Girls become a success, they believe they will gain major material wealth. That is the ultimate dream for The Cheetah Girls, fame and fortune.

In the novels, a materialistic mentality is reinforced by peers but also by some adult authority figures. For instance, their vocal coach, Drinka Champagne, is a former successful disco singer, and she tells them "You have got to have a theme and a dream and a mind like a money machine" (*Wishing* 77) to be successful in the music industry. Hip-hop artists' depictions of a glamorous lifestyle increase their popularity and celebrity status in the eyes of young listeners/viewers; consequently, the hip-hop artist/celebrity becomes a role model, someone to emulate if one wants to become accepted, influential, popular, and wealthy. "[T]he expansion of celebrity status in contemporary culture is dependent on its association with both capitalism, where the celebrity is an effective means for the commodification of the self, and democratic sentiments, where the celebrity is the embodiment of the potential of an accessible culture" (Marshall 25–26).

Thus, we see the phenomenal ratings of a television show like *American Idol*, where unknown yet occasionally talented dreamers can become overnight celebrities and reap the rewards. For children and young adults, who are just beginning to form their own identities alongside their growing desire to belong, the desire to be a celebrity—famous, popular, and rich—becomes an intoxicating dream. According to David Giles in *Illusions of Immortality*, there is a difference between "fame" and "celebrity"; they "are not strictly interchangeable" (3). Fame, Giles suggests, is a state that has existed throughout history and connected to those who have achieved worldly or spiritually worthy achievements that have impacted the world while "the defining characteristic of celebrity is that it is essentially a *media production*, and its usage is largely confined to the twentieth century" (3–4). In other words, the celebrity (actor, singer, etc.) is a agent/vehicle that multimedia industries (film, television, and music) use to sell products, the latest CD, film, or television show—not to mention endorsements of other consumer items such as perfume, cars, and soft drinks. At the same time, the celebrity is a product in and of him/herself; his or her talent, personality, or intangible "it" quality enables the individual to gain, and hopefully maintain, fame by constantly appealing to the audience/consumers. The celebrity increases his/her visibility by appearing on talk shows, doing radio interviews, and giving cover stories to magazines that sell their products and the celebrity him/herself. The individual who becomes a celebrity is often a willing participant in this marketing game; she or he desires the adulation and wealth.

America, arguably, has become a celebrity/popular culture nation, purchasing tabloids and watching entertainment news shows at a high rate. Reality shows like *Survivor* and *Big Brother* create the opportunity for "nobodies" to gain their fifteen minutes of fame while others like *America's Next Top Model* offer struggling wannabes the opportunity to gain lucrative careers and international stardom.[13] This desire for fame and fortune must fill a spiritual and/or psychological void in the lives of the American public; my interest is in what need does this desire to be famous meet for the protagonists in *The Cheetah Girl* series and for African American girls in general.

Giles speculates that marginalized peoples' "[desire for celebrity] may reflect the desire for success in a culture within which [they] [feel] estranged" (41). To support his claim, Giles notes that there are "(statistically) unexpectedly high numbers of Jewish Nobel Prize winners and, in more recent times still, the over-representation of Afro-Caribbeans and African-Americans in specific fields such as sport and pop music in Europe and America" (41). While this is only one theory of the desire for celebrity,[14] it is an intriguing one for this study, especially when one looks at the celebrated history of African Americans in the areas of athletics and entertainment.

In the United States, African Americans were allowed access into the music industry early on because of the money they could earn media producers and companies while often not reaping the full profits of their works. Vocal skills have given many African Americans a career and a podium on which to speak about important issues of their time. "Popular culture has for many years provided a legitimate setting for the fantasy—from the boxing ring to the music hall and vaudeville to television—especially for members of the working class. [...] [T]he attraction of this fantasy is its inferred capacity to free the individual from their class placement: specifically, they could escape their identification with the working class without defecting to the middle class" (Turner 61). Therefore, they do not provide any space for them to be called a class or ethnic identity deserter. African Americans, many of them from the working class and underclass, have used entertainment and athletics to escape poverty and to provide for their families. African American basketball players, football players, and rappers are some of the latest incarnations of this legacy. Athletics and entertainment are their chance for success and a way to navigate through a society that generally oppresses minorities. Along with this is the desire to become a "somebody;" in the seekers' eyes, celebrity culture fulfills these needs.

The "bling-bling" attitude of current hip-hop artists exemplifies this need to be identified, validated as "somebody;" "Look at me I am important." The Cheetah Girls emulate them. Though most of them come from privileged economic backgrounds, they still desire fame. After giving a performance for the Kats and Kittys, they revel in the audience's approval. "The clapping doesn't stop. [...] we take our bows, and lift our masks off, and throw kisses, just like we planned" (*Wishing* 118). Galleria, in particular, expresses her desire for wealth and fame; Dorinda describes her as "Cheetah number one" (*Bounce* 271).

Galleria is the leader of The Cheetah Girls, and her desire for the group to succeed is what keeps them together. Galleria is also a song writer and, at times, has to cajole the girls to sing her songs when they perform, especially in the beginning when the other girls mostly want to sing covers. Her yearning for the spotlight is highlighted during this conflict when she thinks to herself: "when we sing *my* songs—and we are gonna sing *my* songs—there's only gonna be one lead singer: and that's me" (*Wishing* 71). Also in, *Who's 'Bout to Bounce?*, Dorinda is tempted to "bounce" or leave The Cheetah Girls to become a background dancer for a major teen recording artist. Dorinda is arguably the best dancer in the group. And, although she decides to remain with the group, she is attracted to the chance to prove her individual abilities and to become noted as a dancer when Cheetah Girl fame seems slow to materialize.

To ensure commercial success and fame, the Cheetah Girls have studied popular and hip-hop culture. "See, you have to have a catchy name for a group, and a theme" (*Wishing* 79). (Their group's name, The Cheetah Girls, is catchy and also implies a type of wildness that can be associated with sexual aggression; I will articulate this point when I discuss the types of musical groups Gregory bases the Cheetah Girls on.) They are very astute and know what types of images and songs work in the mainstream marketplace. For instance, they based themselves on the now-defunct girl group Destiny's Child and former African

American solo artists like Brandy and Monica. In the novels, Destiny's Child is Karma's Children; Galleria describes them like this: "Karma's Children are four fly singers—Backstabba, Greedi, Peace, and Luvbug—from Houston and they must have instant karma because they had a hit record right out of the box, 'Yes, Yes, Yes.' From what I can see, you don't have to have a lot of lyrics to be large" (*Wishing* 15). Galleria is impressed by Karma's Children' instant success; this is consistent with a society dominated by instant gratification. Early in the series, she even says, "I have to get my songs copyrighted so no one will bite my flavor before I become famous—which is going to happen any second" (*Wishing* 8). She and the other girls know it takes work to become successful, yet when they see other young girls becoming huge superstars seemingly overnight, they are going to feel like failures if they do not find success soon. One wonders if this would be the case for actual African American girls as well.

In addition, when Galleria says, "you don't have to have a lot of lyrics to be large," she seems to be saying that a group doesn't have to be really talented to become famous too. Sometimes in the celebrity world image and packaging trump actual substance, a la Paris Hilton. Yet, because image can change once a nubile face and body age or once the public's interest turns to the next "hot" group or trend, fickle public opinion is not the foundation on which young African American girls, already susceptible to the influence of westernized standards of beauty and accomplishment, should learn to base their self-worth.

Additionally, it is unfortunate that The Cheetah Girls look up to fictional artists based on real groups like Destiny's Child. The talented young women of Destiny's Child were known for wearing some risqué outfits and singing some racy lyrics. For example, in their song, "Jumpin' Jumpin'," the chorus is, "Ladies leave your man at home/The club is full of ballers and/They pockets full grown/And all you fellas leave you girl/With her friends/Cause its eleven thirty and the club is/Jumpin' jumpin'" (From Lyrics007 website). Here, young girls (and young boys) learn that it is okay to cheat on a mate, leaving them at home to go party at a club and to be attracted to men whose "pockets full grown," which implies that girls should seek only boys/men who have money and/or are well endowed. Additionally, the videos of the young women of Destiny's Child also fit into the image of portraying women as sexual objects discussed earlier. By consciously basing The Cheetah Girls on groups like Destiny's Child and having young readers clearly recognize the connection, Gregory is reinforcing the notion that young girls can be successful if they are willing to at least partially exploit their bodies. At times, *The Cheetah Girls* books give contradictory messages, and these are not messages that young African American girls, in particular, need to learn.

The hip-hop-infused *Cheetah Girls* series is a fun read for young African American girls; however, there are underlining messages in the texts that must be addressed. While Gregory's works exhibit positive attributes of hip-hop culture (ethnic unity and collaboration), they also contain and even endorse some negative attributes (problematic sense of self-esteem through materialism and fame) of hip-hop culture that can be detrimental to the emotional, psychological, or social development of African American girls. Whether Gregory's young readers dream of becoming actors, doctors, teachers, or singers, the message that these young girls should be given is that they will be successful because they are sharing their talents, glamorous or not, with the world.

Conclusion

Like writers of the past, many contemporary writers of African American children's and young adult literature continue to take on the responsibility of teaching cultural awareness and self-confidence to their readers because, unfortunately, many of the same problems—racism and discrimination—still exist and challenge their readers' psychological well-being. The task of the writers of African American children's literature has always been and continues to be daunting yet fulfilling. Whether they produce a biography of Harriet Tubman or create a fictional work about time travel, these writers offer African American girls an opportunity to expand their minds as they present protagonists that look, sound, and act like real-life girls, which validates the lived experiences of such girls. My analyses of representational texts by Candy Dawson Boyd, Rita Williams-Garcia, Deborah Gregory, Rosa Guy, Virginia Hamilton, Mildred Pitts Walter, and Jacqueline Woodson in *Just Us Girls: The Contemporary African American Young Adult Novel* illustrate this.

While these writers' protagonists deal with "universal" female experiences that take place during the maturation process, they also contend with the emotional and psychological impact of "race," gender, and class. For these writers, developing strong cultural identities is the way for African American girls to learn how to handle these pressures. Whether their novels' protagonists must confront the death of a loved one, determine their sexual orientation, or venture into inter-racial relationships, they all must first acknowledge and/or develop strong cultural identities in order to successfully traverse their bildungsroman journey.

These writers are also keen observers of present-day American society. They are well aware that contemporary African American girls live in a diverse society and come from various socio-economic and ethnic backgrounds. Therefore, they depict characters who struggle to figure out who they are as individuals and what it means to be *African* American in a postmodern world—struggles many African American girls experience, and thereby, identify with. Oftentimes, as demonstrated in their work, the writers reveal that in order for the protagonists, and African American girls, to overcome these complex identity issues they must learn about their own culture, abandon negative characteristics of white American culture such as the western beauty aesthetic, and incorporate the positive elements of both cultures into their lives.

Because many of these writers recognize the multiplicity of African American identities in the post-Civil Rights era, they stress the need for resilient cultural identities and create characters who struggle to establish individual identities within their cultural communities. In doing so, contemporary writers openly recognize that postmodern, ethnic identity in the United States is based on constructing a liminal hybrid one. As African American women, particularly those who have lived through the post-Civil Rights experience, begin and/or continue to write young adult literature for girls, we will see more examinations of young female protagonists who embrace their common cultural heritage yet also seek to establish individual identities as members of a multiethnic society.

Finally, in the Introduction to this text, I lamented not having access to young adult novels written by African American women when I was a kid. One of my motivations for writing this book is that it will better inform parents and educators alike about the existence of such young adult novels and encourage them to buy them for their children and teach them in their classrooms. I also want to join other academic scholars who see the literary and social value in African American children's/young adult literature and who provide literary criticism, thereby, continuing to elevate the status of this literature in the academy. Consequently, I hope that this book and others like it will increase the mainstream exposure of African American children's/young adult books and their authors and that this generation of African American girls, and subsequent ones, will have unlimited access to books that convey and authenticate their lives.

Notes

Introduction

1. *Bildungsroman* is a German term that describes a genre of writing in which the protagonist's desire "fuels the hero with activity and aggression and prompts him to venture out into the world seeking his own path in life"; "[T]he strength of his initial desire often equals his ultimate amount of social and personal power" (Kester 94). In other words, the protagonist in a Bildungsroman is often in conflict with society's convictions and believes that society, as represented by other characters and by institutions, is at odds with him as well. For a detailed history of the Bildungsroman genre from its German origins, see Todd Knotje's *The German Bildungsroman: History of a National Genre.* Columbia, SC: Camden House, 1993.
2. For more information on the black Bildungsroman, see Geta Le Seur's *Ten Is the Age of Darkness: The Black Bildungsroman.* Columbia: UP of Missouri, 1995; and Gunilla Theander Kester's *Writing the Subject: Bildung and the African American Text.* New York: Peter Lang, 1995.
3. For an example of the complicated identity of African American women in the United States due to their inheritance of slavery, see Hortense J. Spillers' "Mama's Baby, Papa's Maybe: An American Grammar Book." *Diacritics* 17: 2 (1987): 65–81.
4. The "Children of the Sun" chapter of Jennifer Ritterhouse's *Growing Up Jim Crow: How Black and White Southern Children Learned Race* offers a solid discussion of how and initially why this learning process took place.
5. Du Bois had several goals for this magazine series. In *Telling Tales*, Dianne Johnson points out that the first three are particularly important for purposes of teaching young African American children cultural and personal pride. "(a) To make colored children realize that being colored is a normal, beautiful thing, (b) To make them familiar with the history and achievement of the Negro race, and (c) To make them know that other colored children have grown into beautiful, useful and famous persons" (Johnson 18).

6. Rudine Sims Bishop's *Shadow and Substance: Afro-American Experience in Contemporary Children's Fiction* (1982) analyzes the different categories of literature written about and/or for African American children such as "Realistic Fiction with a Social Conscience" and "Culturally Conscious Fiction" and the positive and/or negative influence it has on children and young adults.
7. African American "children's books are cultural products whose existence straddles various realms, including the worlds of education, entertainment, illustrations, and literature. Further, this kind of literature appeals to our basic human needs for storytelling and story hearing . . . . We utilize children's books as agents of socialization, politicization, and of formal education" (Johnson 1).

Chapter 1

1. Another book that discusses ethnic communities is Bonnie TuSmith's *All My Relatives: Community in Contemporary Ethnic American Literature*. Ann Arbor: UP of Michigan, 1993.
2. Stepto's concept of "ritual grounds" can also be applied to other ethnic groups such as Native Americans' reservations, Chinese Americans' Chinatowns, and Chicanos' barrios.
3. Other works of fiction in the African American Literature canon that discuss island culture include, Gloria Naylor's *Mama Day* and Ntozake Shange's *Sassafrass, Cypress, and Indigo*.
4. He also seems to trigger her sexuality. Martha's "pulse quickened" when she thinks of him. She is in the middle of her maturation process and though she is not interested in the island boy, Beau, whom many islanders expect her to marry, she is interested in Hal. Hal represents the unknown and the outside world she wants to know. This is part of the attraction.
5. "There are social pressures on ethnics to conform to habits, beliefs and values" (Bruhn 57).
6. Walter uses African American vernacular tradition throughout her text. An example is her portrayal of Titay's folk ways, diction, and storytelling abilities. At one point, Walter has Titay tell a folktale that is loosely based on a tale from Zora Neale Hurston's *Mules and Men*.
7. Martha is conscious not to further alienate herself from her community by using Standard English. "She wished her teacher could understand why it was so difficult for her to talk words that she wrote. What would the women think if she went around saying: *I do not … he does … she is … you are? That I'm crazy*, she thought. Then she remembered Ocie words: … *got no time fuh yo friends no mo … you always thought you better'n us*. She knew she would never talk book talk in front of those women, no matter what Miss Boudreaux said" (91).

8. Joyce is forced to realize that Cindy and Jay-Jay are only "pretending to be [her] friend[s] (sic)" (44) when they betray a secret that she tells them—that she likes Andre, a popular boy at school. When he openly rejects Joyce, even calling her a "cow" (40), Cindy and Jay-Jay laugh at "his loud put-down" (40).

Chapter 2

1. Will Smith's now defunct television series, *The Fresh Prince of Bel-Air*, provides the example of Will as an authentic black who grew up in urban Philadelphia. He wears hip-hop fashions with flair and commands the language of the hip-hop culture with expert timing and effect. The audience is encouraged to view Will as the geniune representative, a real voice from the African American youth culture group, in contrast to his cousin, Carlton. Carlton dresses conservatively or "white" in argyle sweaters, cannot perform the latest hip-hop dances, idealizes the white singer, Tom Jones, and holds many conservative social and political views that are not a part of the African American collective agenda. When Carlton tries to use the language of the hip hop culture, it sounds stilted and false. Carlton's "non-African American" traits are played for laughs and highlight his displacement from the experiences of the general African American community and lack of knowledge of the codes of blackness.
2. Black and white girls also discuss the effects of racism on their relationships in other Woodson novels such as *I Hadn't Meant to Tell You This* (1994) and *Lena* (1999).
3. As Tiffany says in Rebecca Carroll's *Sugar in the Raw: Voices of Young Black Girls in America*, "I have close white girlfriends at school. They're close, but not *real* close. There is a fine line between close and real close, but I guess what it really comes down to is trust. [...] With my white friends, I don't think about being close or real close, I just know that there is a difference between being close and real close" (138). Sheila, one of the three black girls in *Maizon at Blue Hill*, expresses similar beliefs: "I speak to some [white girls] and some of them are cool and everything. But I know I'm not going to make any of those tight friends you grow old with like I've made with Charli and Marie" (Woodson 93).
4. Twine says in "Brown-Skinned White Girls: Class, Culture, and the Construction of White Identity in Suburban Communities" that biracial girls of African descent who are raised in middle and upper-middle class suburban communities with white mothers [and I would argue in a single-parent home with a white parent], develop culturally white identities. Most of the girls in her study lost their racial neutrality and gained a Black consciousness only after entering the University of California at Berkeley and encountering diverse ethnic groups (216–217).
5. Woodson's *The House You Pass on the Way* protagonist, Staggerlee, also has to think about how her parents' interracial marriage and intra-racial discrimination affect her familial and social life. The fact that her mother is white is one of the reasons she loses her best friend, Hazel. One of the black girls tells Hazel, "[S]he got a white mama,

Hazel. [...] [A]nd her mother thinks she's better than everyone too—just cause she's white" (24). Staggerlee tries to explain that her mother is a quiet person and that that is the reason she rarely speaks to anyone. Nevertheless, the girls convince Hazel that Staggerlee is a snob, and Hazel is no longer her friend.

Chapter 3

1. See, for example, Chesnutt, Charles W. *The Wife of His Youth and Other Stories of the Color Line*. 1899. Ridgewood, NJ: The Gregg Press, 1967; Fauset, Jessie Redmon. *Plum Bun*. 1928. Boston: Beacon Press, 1990; Larson, Nella. *Passing*. 1929. New York: Penguin Books, 1997; Thurman, Wallace. *The Blacker the Berry*. London: The X Press, 1997. A sampling of sociological interest in the subject of the effect of images of black female beauty are: White, Walter. "Paradox of Color." *The New Negro*. Ed. Alain Locke. 1925. New York: Touchstone, 1992. 361–368; Frazier, Franklin E. *Black Bourgeoisie*. Glencoe, Illinois, 1957; Grier, Williams and Price M. Cobb. *Black Rage*. New York: Basic Books, 1968; Bogle, Donald. *Toms, Coons, Mulattoes, Mammies, and Bucks: An Interpretive History of Blacks in American Films*. New York: Viking, 1973; Taylor, Paul C. "Malcolm's Conk and Danto's Colors; or Four Logical Petitions Concerning Race, Beauty, and Aesthetics." *Beauty Matters*. Ed. Peg Zeglin Brand. Bloomington: Indiana UP, 2000. 57–64.
2. In many ways Guy sets up a typical story of socio-economic and intra-racial color discrimination that has been discussed in other literary works such as Dorothy West's *The Wedding* (1995).
3. A literary treatment of this social division occurs in Charles W. Chesnutt's short story, "The Wife of His Youth." Mr. Ryder is a mulatto and a forceful proponent of blue-vein societies and believes that the mulatto elite will eventually be assimilated into the white population. Association with, and, in particular, marriage to darker-skinned African Americans would hinder the social and economic progress of lighter-skinned African Americans. Mr. Ryder says, "[O]ur fate lies between absorption by the white race and extinction in the black. The one doesn't want us yet, but may take us in time. The other would welcome us, but it would be for us a backward step" (Chesnutt 7). For another early version of this issue, see Sutton Griggs' *A Hindered Hand*. 1905. New York: AMS Press, 1969.
4. Elenore van Notten says, "[S]ince the white middle class was likely to reject racially specific physical distinctions and modes of behavior, the emerging black middle class concentrated its efforts on erasing all distinguishing physical features through meticulous matching of partners and the scrupulous emulation of the social codes of their white counterparts. Despite their efforts, the assimilationist aspirations of the black minority were largely unsuccessful. White America, oblivious to black social stratification, perceived blacks only in monolithic terms" (216).

5. In *Ain't I a Beauty Queen?: Black Women, Beauty, and the Poltics of Race*, Maxine Leeds Craig says, "By the end of the decade [1960s], however, dominant gender norms, which were infused with ideals of European beauty, reemerged" (128).
6. For instance, "[T]he paper-bag test involved placing an arm inside a brown paper bag, and only if the skin on the arm was lighter than the color of the bag would a prospective member be invited to attend church services" (Russell, Wilson & Hall 27).
7. Or, as Wallace Thurman more plainly writes in *The Blacker the Berry* (1929), "[A] wife of dark complexion was considered a handicap unless she was particularly charming, wealthy, or beautiful. An ordinary dark woman was no suitable mate for a Negro man of prominence" (44).
8. Dorothy West discussed this issue in *The Wedding* (1995), a novel set in the 1950s. In the novel, several light-skinned African Americans choose not to marry darker-skinned African Americans because of black bourgeois social expectations. Also, another light-skinned character marries and has a child with a dark-skinned African American to her family's disapproval. The novel examines many issues concerning color and class within the African American community.
9. Toni Morrison's classic novel, *The Bluest Eye* (1970), is considered by many scholars to be the definitive contemporary statement on the negative impact of Western beauty ideals on African American girls.
10. "As an outsider herself, Guy could present [her characters'] world with a special sensitivity and compassion. Having grown up black, female, West Indian, and an orphan, she is deeply empathetic and committed to others cast in the role of outsider. Her orphan's experience has given her a unique angle of vision, and her experience as a minority figure, by virtue of both race and cultural background, adds yet another dimension, enhancing her observational skills" (Norris 23).
11. Also, there is a stress on "sisters," particularly darker-skinned women, not brothers being omitted from the social marriage pool. Because the ideal of beauty in the western world is the white woman, African American women cannot meet this ideal and in the Western world a woman's socio-economic capital has been her physical attractiveness. The men, although discriminated against, are not held to the same sort of attractiveness ideal that the women are. As a result, Cathy believes that her Caucasian physical features and light skin should attract all men to her, and Sarah's dark skin should not.
12. When Madam Armand, Jean-Pierre's mother, hears Cathy, Milt, and the others teasing Sarah about her dark complexion, she chastises them and says, "How you talk to your friend so—before strangers? How you talk things about blackness. You do not like us—*que c'est malheureux*—because we are ugly? Or did you want to make pretty Sarah feel ugly? You are not kind" (88).
13. Adolf Hitler vilified Jews during his reign in Nazi Germany and used dehumanizing tactics to "justify" the murders of millions of Jews during the Holocaust.
14. Sharon G. Flake's *The Skin I'm In* (1998) is another young adult novel that discusses intra-racial discrimination and its effects on a young female protagonist.

Chapter 4

1. Fahamisha Patricia Brown in *Performing The Word: African American Poetry as Vernacular Culture* defines the African American vernacular tradition or culture as "the expressive culture of people descended from Africans enslaved in that part of North America that became the United States of America. Their culture was an invention, or reinvention, forged out of historical, sociopolitical, and cultural necessities. Africans from many linguistic and cultural backgrounds because one people separated from the larger community of 'Americans.' African American cultural expression, including literature, also evolved separate from the mainstream of American cultural expression, even as African Americans strived to demonstrate literary competence within that mainstream" (2).
2. In fact, some scholars of children's and young adult literature believe that it is their job to write "scholarly articles and dissertations that remove the 'magic' from children's books" (Harris 275) and to reveal the social, historical, and political aspects of the works. For a more in-depth discussion about the relationship between children's and young adult literature and critical theory, see Jill P. May's text, *Children's Literature and Critical Theory: Reading and Understanding*. New York: Oxford UP, 1995.
3. Rosa Guy also dealt with homosexuality in the young adult novel *Ruby* (1976).
4. See, Jennifer Ritterhouse's *Growing Up Jim Crow: How Black and White Southern Children Learned Race*. Chapel Hill: University of North Carolina Press, 2006. While this work focuses on segregation's "racial etiquette" during the mid-twentieth century, the process in which children learned prejudice then is still useful to understanding how and why racism is passed down from one generation to the next.
5. Woodson explores sexual orientation and acceptance in some of her other works as well. For example, in *The Dear One*, analyzed in Chapter Two, Marion, a friend of Afeni's mother, is a lesbian. Like Afeni's mother, she was close to Rebecca's mother when they were in school at Spelman and wants to help Rebecca. However, Rebecca's mother does not accept Marion's lifestyle and instills her beliefs in her daughter. Rebecca has negative perceptions of lesbians; however, as her friendship with Marion grows, her attitude towards lesbians becomes tolerant.
6. "Homosexuality represents in some cultures a betrayal of family norms, a rejection of ethnic heritage, or a sin. Relatively low rates of disclosure to families have been reported therefore among Asian, African-American, and Latino gay men and lesbians. Lesbian and gay youth from ethnic/racial subcultures have to manage more than one stigmatized identity, often without family support, creating additional stress and isolation" (Perrin 74).
7. "Staggerlee may grow up and settle into gayness, as Woodson did, after experimenting with heterosexual relationships throughout high school. Interestingly, writing in 1995, Woodson said that she did not believe that, in fact, fourteen-year-old lesbians exist, but says she can write about 'a fourteen-year-old girl who struggles with her identity as she watches friends with boys, sees gay couples and fears she may be seeing herself'" (Stover 126).

8. Staggerlee also has to think about how her parents' interracial marriage, her biracial identity, and intra-racial discrimination affect her familial and social life. The fact that her mother is white is the other reason she loses her best friend, Hazel. One of the girls tells Hazel, "[S]he got a white mama, Hazel. [...] [A]nd her mother thinks she's better than everyone too—just cause she's white" (24). Staggerlee tries to explain that her mother is a quiet person and that that is the only reason she rarely speaks to anyone, but the girls convince Hazel that Staggerlee is a snob, and Hazel is no longer her friend. Additionally, Staggerlee does not know any member of her extended family until Trout, a cousin, comes to visit. Her father and his family became estranged when he married her mother, and it is implied that the same happened with her mother's family. However, her father tells Staggerlee and her siblings stories about her activist grandparents and her aunts. In doing so, her father is able to help Staggerlee develop pride in her African American heritage while also acknowledging her white one. Staggerlee has a black consciousness and has come to terms with her biracial heritage. The most significant reason Staggerlee has difficulties establishing relationships though is her sexual orientation.
9. In fact, "[t]he process of 'coming out' is rarely smooth. Teenagers typically begin to disclose their questions about their sexual orientation to close friends—preferably first to a gay or lesbian friend if they know of any who have already 'come out.' [...] Adult role models (e.g., a nurse, a teacher) who are known to be homosexual may be among the first adults to whom a teenager feels sufficiently safe to disclose her/his concerns. Siblings and parents are rarely the first to hear about a teenager's emerging homosexual orientation, because the fear of rejection and approbation is great and the stakes are high" (Perrin 79).
10. "Stagolee ... is the star of the bad men. The several forms his name takes suggest the numerousness of the versions of his story, and those versions reflect a range of attitudes toward this most famous of the badmen: the exaggeratedly bombastic, the boastful, the tragic, the pathetic, the heroic" (Bryant 13).
11. Woodson's own introduction to the Staggerlee legend was positive and influential. In a personal interview, she says, "Staggerlee was introduced to me by a 7th grade English teacher who turned me on to the idea of words being musical and poetic" (Woodson). Therefore, the writer herself has felt empowered by Staggerlee and by the teacher who introduced the legend to her. Consequently, Woodson sees the legend in a positive light and wants to share its inspirational message with her young readers.

Chapter 5

1. For an additional information, see Bernard, Emily, ed. *Some of My Best Friends: Writings on Interracial Friendships*. Harper Collins, 2004.
2. Original source citation as cited by Stover, "Jacqueline Woodson," Retrieved from www.randomhouse.com/teachers.authors/wood.htm on 4 September 2001, 5.

3. Woodson also examines black/white girl relationships in *Maizon in Blue Hill* (1992) and *Between Madison and Palmetto* (1993).
4. As discussed in Chapter 2, codes of blackness, for instance, the specific way urban, working-class blacks speak, are used to construct authentic black group identity. The use of black vernacular is a leading marker of group membership. Interestingly, during the incident in the cafeteria, Lena uses non-Standard English and sounds black because of the way she pronounces words. "[L]iking the way Lena talks— like a black girl almost," Marie thinks, "[F]or a second I wondered it she were light- skinned" and even asks Lena, "Are you black?" (18). Marie's reaction suggests that ethnicity can be performed; otherwise, how could a white girl sound black? A related question, as discussed in Chapter 2, is how can a Black girl act white?
5. Marie does receive postcards from her estranged mother, but she still greatly suffers from the separation.
6. After Lena expresses the futility of working hard in school because she would never be accepted into a college, Marie says, "[F]or the first time I began to understand the privilege I had. My father was a college professor. I never had to worry about money or the future" (95). Obviously, Woodson is offering a reversal of black and white socioeconomic status as often portrayed in young adult novels.
7. In "Telling Secrets and the Possibilities of Flight in *I Hadn't Meant to Tell You This,*" Paula T. Connolly argues that Lena suffers from invisibility in Chauncey because of her socioeconomic status and because of her silent abuse. "This invisibility becomes a sign of Lena's victimization as well. Her vulnerability as a young, poor female is exacerbated not only because she inculcates society's views of her worthlessness, but also because signs of her abuse are ignored by others" (209).
8. Nina Mikkelsen even argues that "we see that a great deal of Talley's attraction to David [is] the more exotic, liberated life he lives and the freedom from racial oppression and poverty that his race affords him. No matter how bad David is, he takes her away at least temporarily from [her] hated underclass condition [into a fantasy world of white acceptance]" (84).

Chapter 6

1. It must be noted that children also experience a similar grief process when they "lose" a parent to divorce. "There are, to be sure, many similarities in the reactions of children to the breakup of the home via these avenues, and similar adjustments that family must make to accommodate to changes in the family structure and role allocations" (Worden 124). Of course, the parent is not literally "dead" in the case of divorce, but the child does experience a separation from his/her parent. In many of the contemporary African American young adult novels I have studied for *Just Us Girls*, the young protagonist must deal with the loss of a parent whether through death or divorce.

2. Toni is angry when Mattie wears the "I Love New York" tee-shirt that Susan gave her when she returned from one of her trips to visit her father in New York because she knows that Mattie did not like Susan a great deal.
3. According to Worden, guilt is also a feeling some children may experience. They may feel responsible for the person's death. Both Mattie and Toni express this sentiment. Mattie says, "For a while I believed that his getting killed was my fault. I made him die. I did something wrong. But I don't believe that now" (*Blessings* 169). Toni says, "Me too. Sometimes I dream that Susan is crossing the street and I'm shouting to her to stop, but she keeps going" (169).
4. Toni is also supported by Raymond, another peer.
5. In fact, their teacher, Mr. Ashby, has had a heart attack earlier in the novel. Mrs. Swallow is his replacement. He lives, but his heart attack and everyone's fears that he might die open Mattie's wounds.
6. Mattie mentions her special place in *Circle of Gold*; it is "the gingko tree she and her father had discovered two years ago" (89) in a city park.
7. In fact, Mattie and Susan were friends but not as close as Toni and Susan.
8. Toni also places breadsticks in the folds of Susan's dress before leaving the church on the day of the funeral. The breadsticks were important to Susan because she lived with her grandparents and rarely saw her father. They represented a sense of closeness to her father.

Chapter 7

1. For more information , see, Tricia Rose's *Black Noise: Rap Music and Black Culture in Contemporary America*. Middletown, CT: Wesleyan University Press, 1994.
2. For more information, see, Dorothy G. Singer's and Jerome L. Singer's *Handbook of Children and the Media*. Thousand Oaks, CA: Sage, 2002.
3. Bakari Kitwana's *Why White Kids Love Hip-Hop: Wankstas, Wiggers, Wannabes, and the New Reality of Race in America* is a source that further explores other ethnicities' interest in rap music and hip hop culture.
4. See, Tricia Rose's *Black Noise: Rap Music and Black Culture in Contemporary America*. Middletown, CT: Wesleyan University Press, 1994. and Nelson George's *Hip Hop America*. New York: Penguin, 1998.
5. See Baraka, Imamu Amiri. *Blues People: Negro Music in White America*. 1963, New York: W. Morrow, 1970.
6. Grandmaster Flash's lyrics to the rap song, "The Message," are considered as a classic example of "old school" rap and its "true" function within the African American community—to give a voice to the voiceless, the urban underclass. The following is the first verse and the chorus. "Broken glass everywhere/People pissing on the stairs, you know they just/Dont care/I cant take the smell, I cant take the noise/Got no money

to move out, I guess I got no choice/Rats in the front room, roaches in the back/ Junkies in the alley with a baseball bat/I tried to get away, but I couldnt get far/Cause the man with the tow-truck repossessed my car." Chorus: "Dont push me, cause I'm close to the edge/I'm trying not to loose my head/Its like a jungle sometimes, it makes me wonder/How I keep from going under." (From *LyricsFreak* website).

7. The airing of Michael Jackson's "Billie Jean" video in 1983 is generally considered the key moment when MTV began to slowly play more African American artists' videos even though the network had been on the air since 1981.
8. It is interesting to note, that many forms of African American music, including the blues and rock 'n roll, have been deemed too dangerous for the American mainstream at some point in time. Granted, some of the topics and diction can be deemed morally questionable at times. However, I think the fact that a marginalized people had the opportunity to express their social, political, economic as well as personal concerns about living as an oppressed people in the United States weighs heavily here.
9. Chang argues that the music industry encouraged a shift from gangsta rap for economic reasons. "At the end of 1992, as Los Angeles still recovered from the Riots, ex-NWA producer Andre 'Dr. Dre' Young dropped *The Chronic* [a monumental album in rap history and a reference to an African-American urban slang word for marijuana]. Television had brought middle America closer to a generation's rage than ever before. [...] *The Chronic* seemed a heaven-sent balm. [...] Dre and Snoop's [a protégé of Dr. Dre better known as Snoop Dogg] video for 'Nothin' But a 'G' Thang' and 'Let Me Ride' drove the album beyond triple platinum. Dre was finally moving up—out of Compton and into the Valley, ... closer to the growing fan base. In a strange, somewhat disquieting way, Dre and Snoop had become reassuring, as if their presence now signified that the difference between the ghetto and the exurbs (sic) needed not be measured in social indicators but in degrees of cool" (419–420).
10. Violet J. Harris believes that Gregory's emphasis on biracial identity can also have a negative impact, encouraging young girls to privilege light-skin and "good" hair. This is dangerous since African American girls are already subjected to western/white media views of beauty. She notes that twin sisters and members of The Cheetah Girls, Aquanette and Anginette, are "rarely referred to as pretty or beautiful, but [the twins] often characterize Galleria, Dorinda, and Chanel in that way" (221). They are the only members who can be considered completely African American. She uses Book 4, *Hey, Ho, Hollywood!* to highlight her point and says, "the twins' ready acknowledgment of their vocal talents contrasted to their constant doubts about their physical beauty: 'And I *guess* we're kind of cute: Angie and I are both brown-skinned, with nice 'juicy' lips and big brown eyes. Still, we're not real pretty, like the rest of the Cheetah girls'" (3). These self-deprecating comments suggest that beautiful Black girls must possess the characteristics of biracial or multiracial females-for example, lighter skin and eye colors and long straight or curly hair–to be attractive" (221–222).

11. It is also important to note that producers selected the popular, young adult Raven Symone to portray Galleria in *The Cheetah Girls* movies. Symone, who is also the star of her own Disney television show, *That's So Raven,* has been often praised by parents and critics for demonstrating a "healthy" body image for young girls.
12. This is a reference to Suze Orman's best-selling, financial advice book, "*The Money Book for the Young, Fabulous, and Broke.*" New York: Riverhead, 2005.
13. This "fame" desire is not only an American issue, it is also international. Versions of these shows and others have been very successful in European markets as well. It has been documented by British researchers that young Britons desire fame as an actual career goal, too.
14. See, Graeme Turner's *Understanding Celebrity*. Thousand Oaks, CA: Sage, 2004.

Works Cited

Introduction

Bishop, Rudine Sims. "Walk Tall in the World: African American Literature for Today's Children." *The Journal of Negro Education*. 59.4 (Autumn 1990): 556–565.

Collier, Marta D. "Through the Looking Glass: Harnessing the Power of African American Children's Literature." *The Journal of Negro Education*. 69.3 (Summer 2000): 235–242.

Harris, Violet. "Benefits of Children's Literature." *The Journal of Negro Education*. 59.4 (Autumn 1990): 538–539.

Henderson, Mae Gwendolyn. "Speaking in Tongues: Dialogics, Dialectics, and the Black Women Writer's Literary Tradition." *Changing Our Own Words: Essays on Criticism, Theory, and Writing by Black Women*. Ed. Cheryl A. Wall. New Brunswick: Rutgers UP, 1989. 16–37.

Henderson, Virginia M. "The Development of Self-esteem in Children of Color." *The Multicolored Mirror: Cultural Substance in Literature for Children and Young Adults*. Ed. Merri V. Lindgren. Fort Atkinson, WI: Highsmith Press, 1991. 15–30.

Johnson, Dianne. *Telling Tales: The Pedagogy and Promise of African American Literature for Youth*. New York: Greenwood Press, 1990.

Johnson, Dianne and Catherine E. Lewis. "Introduction: [Children's and Young-Adult Literature]." *African American Review* 32.1 (1998): 5–7.

Kester, Gunilla Theander. *Writing the Subject: Bildung and the African American Text*. New York: Peter Lang Publishing, 1995.

Le Seur, Geta. *Ten Is the Age of Darkness: The Black Bildungsroman*. Columbia: UP of Missouri, 1995.

Smith, Karen Patricia, Ed. Introduction. *African-American Voices in Young Adult Literature: Tradition, Transition, Transformation*. Metuchen, NJ: The Scarecrow Press, 1994. xi–xxx.

Woodson, Jacqueline. "How do I come home again?" *The Horn Book Magazine*. 83.2 (March–April 2007): 119–126.

Zoppa, Linda J. "Color and Class: An Exploration of Responses in Four African-American Coming-of-Age Novels." *African-American Voices in Young Adult Literature: Tradition, Transition, Transformation*. Ed. Karen Patricia Smith. 1994. Metuchen, NJ: The Scarecrow Press, 2001. 169–191.

Chapter 1

Bruhn, John G. "Common Ties: Immigrant and Ethnic Communities." *The Sociology of Community Connections*. New York: Kluwer Academic/Plenum, 2005. 49–72.

Hurston, Zora Neale. *Their Eyes Were Watching God*. 1937. New York: Harper and Row, 1990.

Johnson, Dianne. *Telling Tales: The Pedagogy and Promise of African American Literature for Youth*. New York: Greenwood, 1990.

Stepto, Robert B. *From Beyond the Veil: A Study of Afro-American Narrative*. 1979. Chicago: UP of Illinois, 1991.

Walter, Mildred Pitts. *Trouble's Child*. New York: Lothrop, Lee & Shepard, 1985.

———. Interview. *Broken Silences: Interviews with Black and White Women Writers*. Ed. Shirley M. Jordan. New Brunswick, NJ: Rutgers University Press, 1993. 271–284.

Williams-Garcia, Rita. *Blue Tights*. 1988. New York: Puffin, 1996.

———. Interview. *Broken Silences: Interviews with Black and White Women Writers*. Ed. Shirley M. Jordan. New Brunswick, NJ: Rutgers University Press, 1993. 302–322.

Zoppa, Linda J. "Color and Class: An Exploration of Responses in Four African-American Coming of Age Novels." *African-American Voices in Youth Adult Literature: Tradition, Tranisition, Transformation*. Ed. Karen Patricia Smith. 1994. Metuchen, NJ: The Scarecrow Press, 2001. 169–191.

Chapter 2

Belluck, Pam. "Reason Is Sought for Lag by Blacks in School Effort." *New York Times* 4 July 1999: A1+.

Bishop, Rudine Sims. "Reframing the Debate about Cultural Authenticity." *Stories Matter: The Complexity of Cultural Authenticity in Children's Literature*. Eds. Dana L. Fox and Kathy G. Short. Urbana. IL: National Council of Teachers of English, 2003. 25–37.

———. "Books From Parallel Cultures: New African-American Voices." *Horn Book* (Sept. 1999): 616–620.

Carroll, Rebecca. *Sugar in the Raw: Voices of Young Black Girls in America*. New York: Three Rivers Press, 1997.

DeVos, George A. *Social Cohesion and Alienation: Minorities in the United States and Japan*. Boulder: Westview Press, 1992.

Favor, J. Martin. *Authentic Blackness: The Folk in the New Negro Renaissance.* Durham: Duke UP, 1999.

Greenfield, Eloise. "Writing for Children—A Joy and a Responsibility." *The Black American in Books for Children: Readings in Racism.* Ed. Donnarae MacCann. 1972. Metuchen, NJ: The Scarecrow Press, 1985. 19–22.

Howard, Elizabeth Fitzgerald. "Authentic Multicultural Literature for Children: An Author's Perspective." *The Multicultural Mirror: Cultural Substance in Literature for Children and Young Adults.* Ed. Merri V. Lindgren. Fort Atkinson, WI: Highsmith Press, 1991. 91–99.

Lewis, Amanda E. *Race in the Schoolyard: Negotiating the Color Line in Classrooms and Communities.* New Brunswick, NJ: Rutgers UP, 2003.

Ogbu, John U. *Black American Students in an Affluent Suburb: A Study of Academic Disengagement.* Mahwah, NJ: Lawrence Erlbaum Associates, 2003.

Sebald, Hans. *Adolescence: A Social Psychological Analysis.* Englewood Cliffs, NJ: Prentice Hall, 1992.

Simpson, Andrea Y. *The Tie That Binds: Identity and Political Attitudes in the Post-Civil Rights Generation.* New York: New York UP, 1998.

Stepto, Robert B. *From Behind the Veil: A Study of Afro-American Narrative.* 1973. Chicago: UP of Illinois, 1991.

Stover, Lois Thomas. *Jacqueline Woodson: "The Real Thing."* Lanham, MD: The Scarecrow Press, Inc., 2003.

Twine, Frances Winddance. "Brown-Skinned White Girls: Class, Culture, and the Construction of White Identity in Suburban Communities." *Displaying Whiteness: Essays in Social and Cultural Criticism.* Ed. Ruth Frankenberg. Durham: Duke UP, 1997. 214–243.

Woodson, Jacqueline. *The Dear One.* New York: Bantam Doubleday, 1991.

———. *Maizon at Blue Hill.* New York: Bantam Doubleday, 1992.

———. *Between Madison and Palmetto.* New York: Yearling Book, 1993.

———. *The House You Pass on the Way.* New York: Bantam Doubleday, 1997.

———. Personal Email. 15 May 2001.

Zoppa, Linda J. "Color and Class: An Exploration of Responses in Four African-American Coming-of-Age Novels." *African American Voices in Young Adult Literature: Tradition, Transition, Transformation.* Ed. Karen Patricia Smith. 1994.

Chapter 3

Chesnutt, Charles W. "The Wife of His Youth." *The Wife of His Youth and Other Stories of the Color Line.* 1899. Ridgewood, NJ: The Gregg Press, 1967.

Craig, Maxine Leeds. *Ain't I a Beauty Queen?: Black Women, Beauty, and the Politics of Race.* New York: Oxford UP, 2002.

Cross, William E., Jr., and Peony Fhagen-Smith. "Patterns of African American Identity Development: A Life Span Perspective." *New Perspectives on Racial Development: A Theoretical and Practical Anthology.* Eds. Charmaine L. Wijeyesinghe and Bailey W. Jackson III. New York: New York UP, 2001. 243–270.

Edwards, Korie, Katrina M. Carter-Tellison, and Cedric Herring. "For Richer, for Poorer, Whether Dark or Light: Skin Tone, Marital Status, and Spouse's Earning." *Skin Deep: How Race and Complexion Matter in the "Color-Blind" Era.* Eds. Cedric Herring, Verna Keith, and Hayward Derrick Horton. Chicago: UP of Illinois, 2004. 65–81.

Elder, Arlene. *The Hindered Hand: Cultural Implications of Early African-American Fiction.* Westport, CT: Greenwood Press, 1978.

Frazier, E. Franklin. *Black Bourgeoisie.* Glencoe, IL: The Free Press, 1957.

Guy, Rosa. *The Music of Summer.* New York: Delacorte Press, 1992.

Hunter, Margaret L. Race, *Gender, and the Politics of Skin Tone.* New York: Routledge, 2005.

Lakoff, Robin Talmach and Raquel L. Scherr. *Face Value: The Politics of Beauty.* Boston: Routledge, 1984.

Morrison, Toni. *The Bluest Eye.* 1970. New York: Plume, 1994.

Norris, Jerrie. *Presenting Rosa Guy.* Boston: Twayne Publishers, 1988.

Russell, Kathy, Midge Wilson, and Ronald Hall. *The Color Complex.* New York: Harcourt, 1992.

Thurman, Wallace. *The Blacker the Berry.* 1929. London: The X Press, 1997.

van Notten, Elenore. *Wallace Thurman's Harlem Renaissance.* Atlanta: Rodopi, 1994.

Williamson, Joel. *New People: Miscegenation and Mulattoes in the United States.* Baton Rouge: Louisiana State UP, 1995.

Zoppa, Linda J. "Color and Class: An Exploration of Responses in Four African-American Coming of Age Novels." *African-American Voices in Youth Adult Literature: Tradition, Transition, Transformation.* Ed. Karen Patricia Smith. 1994. Metuchen, NJ: The Scarecrow Press, 2001. 169–191.

Chapter 4

Blume, Judy, Ed. *Places I Never Meant to Be: Original Stories by Censored Writers.* New York: Simon & Schuster, 1999.

Brown, Fahamisha Patricia. *Performing the Word: African American Poetry as Vernacular Culture.* New Brunswick, NJ: Rutgers UP, 1999.

Bryant, Jerry H. *"Born in a Mighty Bad Land": The Violent Man in African American Folklore and Fiction.* Bloomington, IN: Indiana UP, 2003.

Harris, Violet J. "'May I Read This Book?' Controversies, Dilemmas, and Delights in Children's Literature." *Battling Dragons: Issues and Controversy in Children's Literature.* Ed. Susan Lehr. Portsmouth, NH: Heinemann, 1995. 275–283.

Lehr, Susan. *Battling Dragons: Issues and Controversy in Children's Literature*. Portsmouth, NH: Heinemann, 1995.

Levine, Lawrence W. *Black Culture and Black Consciousness: Afro-American Folk Thought from Slavery to Freedom*. New York: Oxford UP, 1977.

Perrin, Ellen C. *Sexual Orientation in Child and Adolescent Health Care*. New York: Kluwer Academic/Plenum, 2002.

Rudman, Masha Kabakow. *Children's Literature: An Issues Approach*. 1976. White Plains, NY: Longman, 1995.

Stover, Lois Thomas. *Jacqueline Woodson: "The Real Thing."* Lanham, MD: Scarecrow, 2003.

Woodson, Jacqueline. *The House You Pass on the Way*. New York: Bantam Doubleday, 1997.

———. Personal E-mail. 15 May 2001.

———. Interview. *Booklist*. 101.1 (February 1, 2005): 968.

Chapter 5

Carroll, Rebecca. *Sugar in the Raw: Voices of Young Black Girls in America*. New York: Three Rivers, 1997.

Connolly, Paula T. "Telling Secrets and the Possibilities of Flight in *I Hadn't Meant to Tell You This*." *Exploring Culturally Diverse Literature for Children and Adolescents: Learning to Listen in New Ways*. Eds. Darwin L. Henderson and Jill P. May. New York: Pearson, 2005. 205–215.

Hamilton, Virginia. *A White Romance*. New York: Scholastic, 1987.

hooks, bell. *Black Looks: Race and Representation*. Boston: South End, 1992.

Mikkelsen, Nina. *Virginia Hamilton*. New York: Twayne, 1994.

Morrison, Toni. *The Bluest Eye*. 1970. New York: Plume, 1994.

Stover, Lois Thomas. *Jacqueline Woodson: "The Real Thing."* Lanham, MD: Scarecrow, 2003.

Tatum, Beverly Daniel. *"Why Are All the Black Kids Sitting Together in the Cafeteria?": And Other Conversations About Race*. 1997. New York: Basic Books, 2003.

Woodson, Jacqueline. *I Hadn't Meant to Tell You This*. New York: Laurel-Leaf Books, 1994.

———. *Lena*. New York: Dell Laurel-Leaf, 1999.

———. Personal E-mail. 15 May 2001.

Chapter 6

Boyd, Candy Dawson. *Circle of Gold*. New York: Scholastic, 1984.

———. *Breadsticks and Blessing Places*. New York: Macmillan, 1985.

Silverman, Phyllis Rolfe. *Never Too Young to Know: Death in Children's Lives*. New York: Oxford UP, 2000.

Worden, J. William. *Children and Grief: When a Parent Dies*. New York: Guilford, 1996.

Chapter 7

Chang, Jeff. *Can't Stop Won't Stop: A History of the Hip-Hop Generation.* New York: Picador, 2005.

Giles, David. *Illusions of Immortality: A Psychology of Fame and Celebrity.* New York: St. Martin's, 2000.

Gregory, Deborah. *The Cheetah Girls: Livin' Large, Books 1–4.* New York: Jump at the Sun, 1999.

Harris, Violet J. "*The Cheetah Girl Series*: Multiracial Identity, Pop Culture, and Consumerism." *Exploring Culturally Diverse Literature for Children and Adolescents.* Eds. Darwin L. Henderson and Jill P. May. New York: Pearson, 2005. 216–228.

Kitwana, Bakari. *Why White Kids Love Hip-Hop: Wankstas, Wiggers, Wannabes, and the New Reality of Race in America.* New York: Basic Civitas, 2005.

Marshall, P. David. *Celebrity and Power: Fame in Contemporary Culture.* Minneapolis: U of Minnesota P, 1997.

Pough, Gwendolyn D. *Check It While I Wreck It: Black Womanhood, Hip-Hop Culture, and the Public Sphere.* Boston: Northeastern UP, 2004.

Powell, Kevin. "Is Hip-Hop Dead?: 'Hip-hop culture has been murdered.'" *Ebony* (June 2007): 61.

Turner, Graeme. *Understanding Celebrity.* Thousand Oaks, CA: Sage, 2004.

Index